Little Creek

FINDING ELEMENTAL LIFE IN BROWN COUNTY

Daly Walker
Paintings by **Toni Wolcott**

HAWTHORNE PUBLISHING

Grateful acknowledgment is made to *The Southampton Review,*
where "Water" originally appeared. "Fire" was featured in the
Fall 2013 edition of *Catamaran Literary Reader.*

Some sources were available using GFDL conventions though
Massive Multiauthor Collaboration sites.

ISBN 978-0-615-29013-3

Book design and typesetting by Wilson Design, LLC, Indianapolis, Indiana
using font families of Sabon Roman and Cochin.

Published in the United States by
Hawthorne Publishing
15601 Oak Road
Carmel, IN 46033
317-867-5183
www.hawthornepub.com

For my daughters

BETH

SARAH

KATIE

and my grandchildren

TERI

JACQUELINE

SEBASTIAN

CONTENTS

ARRIVAL 9

SHELTER 17

EARTH 31

LIGHT 39

AIR 47

WOOD 55

WATER 63

STONE 75

SOUND 83

FIRE 91

DEPARTURE 99

EPILOGUE 105

The world today is sick to its thin blood
for lack of elemental things, for fire before the hands,
for water welling up from the earth, for air,
for the dear earth itself underfoot...The longer I stayed,
the more eager was I to know this coast and to share
its mysterious and elemental life.

HENRY BESTON
The Outermost House

Nothing endures but change.

HERACLITUS

ARRIVAL

For many years, my family's home was a brick colonial in Columbus, Indiana, where I practiced general surgery. The view from its front windows was of a paradise of meadow, woods, and river. In the backyard there was a sweet gum tree and a lily pond with goldfish, a pool with a slate deck where my three daughters swam, and a garden where I tended flowers. Inside were French posters, original art and oriental rugs, a study with a black leather chair and shelf-lined walls that held all my books, bedrooms where the girls slept and grew. I assumed my life would last indefinitely inside those walls. However, something went wrong that I'm still trying to understand. Lives quaked. A marriage crumbled. All I know is that blaming doesn't help. As Alice Hoffman wrote in *Here on Earth*, "When all is said and done, the weather and love are the two elements about which one can never be sure." The house and its furnishings were lost to me in a divorce. I was left, not only dispossessed, but also depressed and discouraged that I had tried at love and failed, that I had let my family down.

In the three years that followed the separation, I went back in the house once for a couple of hours to collect a few of my things and to stack my books for a mover to box up and deliver to me. I felt like a trespasser in my home, like someone grabbing at keepsakes while fleeing a fire, escaping with his life. The place was so drenched in memory and the ghosts of my girls that it broke my heart. I wept while the house-keeper kept an eye on me. It was peace I wanted, not possessions. I knew for certain forgiveness is healthier than nursing old wounds. I wanted resentments put behind us so Jane, my former wife, and I could get to understanding and forgiveness. Then could come healing and finally gratitude for the many good things the marriage had provided.

There comes a time when you should relinquish the past and let it go. I thought I had resigned myself to losing the home as well as the life of stability, comfort, and prestige it housed. But no matter how hard I tried, I could never completely shed my past. Today if I drive by the house, my heart seizes. The feeling is sorrow tinged with guilt and disbelief. I'm sure the locks have been changed, but I wouldn't go in it even if I could. It would be like going back into the fire I escaped to get a treasure that was just ashes.

Without a house to call my own, I felt more like a Bedouin. No. A Bedouin has a tent. I felt more like a homeless man, a street vagrant. As Thoreau said, "A man wants his own home; it's necessary." Just as an eagle needs a nest, a bee a hive, a muskrat a den, like Thoreau, I needed a roof overhead, a closet to hang my clothes, shelves for my books, rooms for the furniture handed down to me by my parents. More than anything, I needed to transform my life, to simplify and cleanse it of depression, doubt, and regret.

After retirement from my surgical practice, I worked for five years as a primary care doctor in a clinic in Boca Grande, Florida, located on a small barrier island on the Gulf Coast. I treated sunburns and jellyfish stings. I removed fishhooks from anglers and prescribed Viagra. All the while, I missed the operating room. It was in that semi-tropical paradise with its white beaches and afternoon sea breeze that I met Toni Wol-cott, a single woman near my age. A mother of two sons, she was a fine artist who had lived alone on the island for many years. She had put a bout with breast cancer and a troubled marriage to a famous Harvard professor behind her. Slim and elegant, she walked to the village in a wide-brim straw hat with a band of yellow feathers. In her kitchen she kept two finches. She listened to opera while she painted in her studio. Her generosity and fine instincts were plentiful. She read my short story, "I Am the Grass," in the *Atlantic Monthly* and appreciated the writing. I was in awe of her watercolor botanicals and of her. It didn't take long for us to decide we wanted to be together.

While we both prized the easy island life of Boca Grande, we wanted to find a summer home to escape the heat and hurricanes. We were quite loving and content with solitude and each other. We envisioned living together in a dwelling in the woods with land around it and a pond, a place of retreat where Toni could set up her easel and I could find the peace of mind to write my stories. We knew it should be a small house that wouldn't be so unwieldy as to enslave us, a simple cottage where we could be with each other and nature, participating in seasons with their rhythms and particularities. I say this knowing that there is a duality between man and nature, and it can be argued that where man is, nature is no longer. I prefer to believe, however, that a thoughtful conservationist can be integral to the natural world just as blades of wild grass can be woven harmoniously into fabric.

Thus, knowing what the property should be, the question then was—where should it be? Although Toni has lived for years in Florida, she is a Yankee from Connecticut and as New England as lighthouses and lobster boats. Wolcott Park in Essex, Connecticut, is named for her father. I am as Hoosier as grain silos and bass boats. My mother's family, the Dalys, emigrated from Ireland and were among the first settlers of eastern Indiana in the late 1700s. Toni thought Indiana was an Indian reservation. I thought of New England as a football team with a villainous coach and a pretty-boy quarterback. Would we put down roots in her East or my Midwest, or in some utopia yet undiscovered by either of us?

We began our search for a place in which to live the elemental life we hoped for by taking a long motor trip up the east coast. On our odyssey we stayed with friends and family in garden spots. A "mooch trip," Toni called it. Together in the car for two months, we read stories to each other, listened to public radio, or talked while sharing driving duties. I found I could be myself with Toni and still be accepted. Those two months confirmed our compatibility and affirmed that we could trust each other and would get along fine, just the two of us.

ARRIVAL

Along the way, we found the Blue Ridge Mountains of North Carolina scenic and seductive, the coast of Maine with its rugged islands and breakers picturesque, the country roads and red barns of Vermont quaint, the grassy dunes and whaling cottages of Sag Harbor attractive. But something was missing. No place seemed like home. Nothing said to us, "This is where you belong." We decided to look west, specifically as the song says, "back home again in Indiana and the fields I used to roam."

To those who don't know Indiana, the Hoosier state is often thought of as nothing but flat, uninteresting farmland. However, during the ice age, violent geological forces carved up the earth of the southern part of Indiana into the rugged hills and deep valleys of Brown County, with its seemingly endless views of a vast landscape composed of dense hardwood forests. These vistas have, for many years, inspired the painters of its art colony to capture the county's natural beauty on canvas.

As a nine-year-old boy in 1950, I attended Gnaw Bone Camp, a small rustic retreat in the wilderness of Brown County. We lived in tents, collected box turtles and bugs, snared snakes in creek beds, and hiked the forest, learning trees by their bark and leaves and birds by their cry. We built bridges and cabins out of rough-cut native timber and army surplus supplies. At night we gathered around a campfire and listened to ghost stories told by Fred Lorenz, the camp's owner. "Taily pole, taily pole," he would chant in a low, scary voice. "I want my taily pole," or "I'm going to get your liver." I wasn't sure what my liver was for, but the thought of losing it made me quake. A giant rawboned and handsome man in work pants and a white T-shirt, Fred was an easygoing Boy Scout master, a woodworker, a homespun philosopher, and a naturalist, a hero in the eyes of boys without aspiring to be one. I was in awe of Fred and consider him one of the most influential people in shaping my life. He taught me to appreciate the beauty and mystery of those wooded Indiana hills. Because of Fred, a love of nature grabbed hold of me and never let go. It was natural then that during a search for a wilderness retreat, my inner compass would lead me back to Brown County. I wanted Toni to see this Eden of the Midwest. I wanted her to love it as I did and to be inspired by its bucolic beauty. But she was a true-blue Yankee and skeptical of anything beyond the Alleghenies.

ARRIVAL

On a gray windy day in March, Toni and I arrived in Nashville, Indiana, a quaint village in the heart of Brown County's hills. We spent the night in the Artist Colony Inn's four-poster bed. The following day, Melinda, a petite real estate agent, drove us in her Lexus SUV over narrow hilly county roads with names like Grandma Barnes, Bear Wallow, Clay Lick, and Greasy Creek. The landscape was suffused in a dull light that made everything appear drab and worn out. In a striped business suit and heels, Melinda walked carefully, avoiding the mire in the muddy yards of log cabins with split-rail fences and of abandoned bed and breakfast lodges. We saw hot tubs green with algae, paint peeling from ceilings, and the carcass of a deer that had been gutted by a coyote. Toni protested politely. I became discouraged. What happened to my rural fantasy? Where was the beautiful Brown County I wanted her to adore?

Late in the morning, we headed north of Nashville on Helmsburg Road, winding through a narrow peaceful valley where horses grazed in a pasture with a stream running through it. A doe and her fawn loped through the field and disappeared into the trees. Toni spotted an old red barn she wanted to paint. We were seeing the Brown County I had hoped to show her.

After about six miles, we turned right onto Little Creek Drive, a single-lane blacktop, and entered a dense green wilderness.

"This is the place for you," Melinda offered.

Soon the road turned into gravel and washboard. We jostled up a steep hill through dense woods past a run-down house with dark windows and a camper in the driveway. I thought of Appalachia and *Deliverance*. After another half mile the road curved through the front yard of a small, shingled dwelling. In its yard was a wagon wheel and a cow's skull on a post, a chicken coop, an aboveground swimming pool, and an all terrain vehicle. Melinda slowed nearly to a stop, and I thought, *oh no, this can't be it.*

"We're almost there," Melinda said.

She fed the Lexus gas. I breathed a sigh of relief.

The road curved back into the woods. Ahead, I saw the lane narrow and dive steeply down onto the dam of small pond. I thought a slip of a tire would put us in the water. Melinda gripped the steering wheel of the Lexus tightly and made light of the precarious passage over the dam. I looked at Toni, who raised her eyebrows. Melinda headed the car up another hill and deeper into the woods. I exhaled. Around a curve, the road finally straightened and leveled off as it entered an arcade of forest. Just ahead, a mother quail and her covey of chicks fled into the brush. At a tall cairn made of brown stones, Melinda braked the car and announced that this monument marked the beginning of the thirty-acre property she thought was the one we envisioned. Through flitting light and shadows, she drove on slowly, allowing us to admire the landscape on either side of the road. Everywhere were magnificent trees: tall, straight hickories, aspens, oaks, and smooth-barked beeches. The floor of the forest was carpeted with ferns that gave me the feeling that this place had existed since the beginning of time. Suddenly, we arrived at a clearing in the woods. We drove up a slight incline and parked beside a cabin made of dovetailed logs and chinking. It had a steep chalet-like roof and two second-story dormers with large arched windows overlooking the land. Surrounding the deck of the entryway were perennial gardens with clumps of wild grass, purple irises, and a rhododendron bush waiting to bloom. The cabin was flanked by a barn with rough-sawn oak siding and a loft that Melinda suggested would make a perfect artist's studio.

We climbed out of the car. A tide of excitement rose in me. I walked up a stone path that led to a covered veranda that spanned the entire front of the cabin. Before entering the front door, I leaned on the porch railing for a moment and gazed down at the tranquil grassy valley below. There was something poetic about what I saw. There was an open space where our Wheaten Terrier, Oscar Wild, could run and a pond Melinda said was stocked with bass and bluegill. A willow tree and cattails sprouted from its bank. An aging wooden pergola that you might find in a Chinese garden covered a path that led to a dock where a canoe could be moored. In the trees that surrounded the house, birds were chirping, begging to be fed. A rick of firewood left by the previous owner was by the driveway. The neatly stacked logs conjured up an image of wood smoke and a hearth. A warmth spread through me. Water. Stone. Wood. Fire. Air. Shelter. Earth. Sound. Light. The property seemed to be making a promise it would provide all of the elements we were seeking.

Later that day, we bought the thirty acres of quail and quiet, the ponds and peace, the trees and tranquility. The closing was like a birthing ceremony—the beginning of a rich and elemental life. At dinner that evening we christened the property "Little Creek."

As for Shelter, I will not deny that this is now
a necessary of life...Man wanted a home, a place of warmth,
or comfort, first of physical warmth,
then the warmth of the affections.

HENRY D. THOREAU
Walden

SHELTER

Henry Thoreau believed a house should be utilitarian and unadorned, and one should use Yankee shrewdness in choosing where to live "lest after all he find himself in a workhouse, a labyrinth without a clew, a museum, an almshouse, a prison or a splendid mausoleum." While I concede that one's life should not be dominated by luxuries, I believe in living in a house that is architecturally sound and with an interior that is comfortable and pleasant to the eye. To me, a good architect designs buildings that reside unobtrusively in their environment without drawing attention to themselves. It was fitting, then, that the cabin at Little Creek, a house in the woods, was rustic and made of wood. The original structure was a mortised-and-pegged rectangle of 150-year-old, rough-hewn poplar logs. Poplar is the wood of choice for cabins because the trees grow long and straight. The cabin had been notched into the hillside among the trees in the 1980s by Willie Poole, whose family owns the sawmill in the nearby village of Helmsburg. For several years it went unfinished, until the property was purchased by Perry Olds. Perry, an engineer and amateur builder, did much of the work himself. Although the structure was out of plumb and the wiring unprofessional, Perry had an

SHELTER

eye for design. The dormers of the second story he added were nicely symmetrical, with arched windows, and the various rooflines matched as they should. The rough-sawn oak board-and-batten siding on the addition blended well with the original logs, as did the weathered brown shingles. There was a timelessness about the cabin. It looked authentic and homey, like somewhere a man working the land might have lived comfortably with his family a century and a half ago. I can imagine Perry Olds's satisfaction, living in a log home built by his own hand, similar I suppose to the way I once felt as a boy flying a kite that my dad and I had built.

Toni's "Yankee shrewdness" (Thoreau's term seems a bit patronizing. Are Yankees supposed to be shrewder than Hoosiers?) included fine taste and an artist's eye for color and design. She had the front door painted a lively and inviting barn-siding red. When opened, it led into a pine-paneled entryway with a floor of old brick. In the wall space above the door, I hung a large copper pan while Toni held the ladder. As I raised the heavy vessel to its nail, I wobbled precariously. My balance wasn't what it once was. My reaction time had slowed. My strength was on the wane. The little deaths of aging. But also there were little births with my aging, such as enhanced sensitivity to simple experiences.

Under a long vertical window, we placed our prize possession, a Mongolian chest painted cinnabar with gold and green dragons and flowers. We purchased it in Florida at a Sarasota antique store. It was transported with a few other belongings to Indiana by a moving company called "Honeymoon Haulers," a fitting title as we were embarking together on what I thought of as a honeymoon of sorts. Our union wasn't sanctioned by the law of the land or the law of a church, but rather by the law of hearts. I thought of the chest as our common-law wedding gift to each other.

From the entryway, two steps led up to the cabin's main room, which was walled by thick poplar logs cemented together by a chinking of mortar and sand. The most striking feature of the room was the tongue-and-groove cherry floor that gleamed underfoot like a fine piece of furniture. The floors of my Columbus home were also made of cherry. As I walked around the cabin on the polished hardwood, I felt as if I had a recaptured a small part of what was lost from the life I left behind. The floor somehow muted my sense of regret.

One corner of the room served as the kitchen, galley style as in a boat. The appliances were outdated and untrustworthy. The oven didn't work, and only one of the range's four burners was functional. But burgers, grilled vegetables, and chicken kabobs could be prepared on a propane grill on the porch. The small refrigerator was adequate to stockpile perishables. This was critical since the IGA market in Nashville where we did our grocery shopping was several miles away over somewhat treacherous roads. We quickly learned that food stored in the closet-like pantry would be stolen by mice. So flour, sugar, crackers, cereal, and the like were cached in an old oak Hoosier cabinet with tin-lined bins and drawers.

At first, the absence of a dishwasher seemed like an inconvenience. Wouldn't time spent at the sink be better used for something creative or entertaining? But as the Buddhist monk and philosopher, Tich Nhat Hanh, suggested, "Each thought, each action in the sunlight of awareness becomes sacred. In this light, no boundary exists between the sacred and the profane." Part of the transformation I was trying to effect in myself required making moments spent in seemingly meaningless activities meaningful. So each time I attacked a pile of dirty plates and silverware, I concentrated on being aware of the warm water running over my hands, the shape of a dish or spoon, the softness of soap suds. It made the simple task of washing dishes pleasant, something not to be hurried or avoided.

One blue evening in the porch rocker with my wine, I lapsed into nostalgia, recalling places that had sheltered me during my sixty-eight years. The memory of a rooming house in Boulder, Colorado, when I was a summer school student at the university returned a sense of loneliness. A grand, brick fraternity house at Ohio Wesleyan reminded me of breaking away, but with homesickness and a lack of self-confidence. A sandbagged bunker in the Mekong Delta of Vietnam conjured up the horrors of war and the wounds I had seen. It seemed impossible that its violence had been part of my life. I pictured, with fondness, sunsets over the Gulf of Mexico from our family's beach house in Florida. A student bachelor pad in a ghetto of Indianapolis near the medical school and a one-bedroom apartment in Madison, Wisconsin, where I was in residency took me back to tough, lean years of training. I am grateful to have lived in so many places with their wide variety of experiences. My past life seemed full.

For a while, I mused about a chocolate-brown house on Main Street in Winchester, a small county seat town in eastern Indiana. In that cozy cocoon my sister, Sandra, and I grew day by day. Our family home had cedar shake shingles, copper carriage lanterns, a brass knocker on the door, and a sun porch with a paddle fan. My mother was a thinker and social creature who loved to read and give a party. She had a penchant for gold and diamonds and things that glittered. She decorated the interior of the house beautifully with midwestern antiques, Waterford and Steuben crystal, and old wicker. Winston Churchill said, "We shape our buildings, and afterwards our buildings shape us." Mother shaped the house in Winchester, and the house shaped me in ways I don't even realize. I loved living there, the security and comfort of its walls. To me the place was the very idea of home. When my parents aged and weakened, the house was sold. I felt as if a part of me had been amputated, and all I was left with was phantom pain. I wrote a story called "Shadows" about the psychological trauma of the old homestead passing from the family. After all of these years, I still feel as if I live in the shadows of the house's eaves.

While I believe it is a mistake to cling to the past, I also believe you should remember it, learn from it, and honor what's good about it. I was grateful then to be able to furnish our log cabin with my mother's antiques and keepsakes. The living area of the log-walled main room became something of a Walker family museum. A base rocker upholstered in pale orange velvet once belonged to Mother's Aunt Marie in San Francisco. A tall antique secretary with pigeonholes and a fold-out desktop was where Mother wrote her correspondence and paid her bills. Grandmother Bess's old drop-leaf mahogany table and set of brass scales came from her house in Montpelier, Indiana, where both Mother and Daddy were raised in modest homes. An upholstered love seat from Mother's den was positioned in front of the woodstove. It was just large enough for me to sit with Toni and Oscar on a chilly day in front of a fire. The dishes for our meals were Mother's English stoneware, pale aqua plates and cups and saucers, painted with a pattern of birds and flowers. To live in the midst of her belongings conjures up for me a pleasant nostalgia and an image of Mother that is synonymous with my concept of love.

SHELTER

I believe it is important to be, in the words of the Harvard psychiatrist George Valliant, a "keeper of meaning," passing on traditions to the next generations. So someday I will pass on to my daughters their grandmother's belongings and the traditions they represent. I hope my offspring will be able to look at these keepsakes and see me in the way I have come to see my parents, with eyes of compassion, understanding, forgiveness, and gratitude. However, my love of my children is unconditional—tested at times, but unconditional.

Toni and I made the small room adjacent to the main room a den and guest room. We painted the walls a warm shade of mustard yellow. Its furnishings included a hide-a-bed, a wooden chest that served as a coffee table, and a chair covered with cracked and creased leather that had belonged to the funeral director and bank chairman who was my father. He always embarrassed me by introducing me as his "number-one son." For Lord's sake, he had only one son. Plus, who cared who we were? Once constrained by Daddy's admonitions, with old age I have learned to be inspired by his example. It is an honor to sit in the seat of that kind and gentle, self-made, ambitious man. On the partition that separated the den from the living room, we displayed the carved birds we had begun to collect.

While television programs are often violent and vacuous, and to watch them is as mentally nutritional as chewing ice cubes, I purchased a large flat-screen TV. A sports addict and movie buff, I confined my watching to sports and motion pictures as well as *The News Hour* and *Antiques Roadshow* with Toni.

In the center of the cabin's main room, a freestanding stairway with steps made of pine planks rose symbolically to the second floor through a rectangular opening in the ceiling. The bannisters were iron and embellished with sculptured vines. The handles on the doors of a closet were metal cattails of similar design. When the doors were closed, the long slender leaves vibrated and sang as if in a breeze. All of the cabin's hardware was made by a local artisan. He is one of the many painters, potters, and wood and metal sculptors whose studios pepper the hills of Brown County. These artists are as a much a part of the landscape's character as its wildlife and trees.

At the top of the stairs was the master bedroom. We painted its walls sky blue. The windows over the bed were at treetop level. There were times I lay there at night feeling as if Toni and I were children sleeping in a tree house. I would look over at her and with a start realize how radically my life had changed into something solid and elemental. At the same time, an uncertainty would unsettle me. How long will it last? I wonder that, knowing it is better not to dwell on the future.

Along one wall, a large walk-in closet housed our clothes and shoes. Toni and I both have a history of taking pride in what we wear. When I was practicing medicine, I wouldn't have thought of seeing a patient without a sport jacket and a necktie at the collar of my button-down shirt. Toni collected shoes like a Philippine first lady. However, like other aspects of our life at Little Creek, wearing apparel took on a more utilitarian character. To cover our nakedness and keep us warm or shield us from the sun, all we needed were jeans and a flannel shirt or fleece vest when it was cool and khaki shorts and a cotton shirt when it was warm. When we found out how little clothing we required, much of our wardrobe was carted off to Goodwill.

In the bedroom behind the slats of a wooden screen was an alcove that served originally as my office and writing cubicle. Its window offered a view of the land and water below, a landscape that both tranquilized and inspired me.

For the past couple of years, my writing had suffered. Unfocused, tormented, hurt, guilty, depressed, I couldn't concentrate on my work. The words came hard, and when they did, they didn't say much. It was as if all of my senses had been dulled by a strange viral illness that had attacked my cerebral hemispheres. I quit writing for a while, but I missed it. I missed wrestling with a word, a feeling, or an idea. I missed scrutinizing matters and finding out what I really thought and felt. I hoped that by coming to this quiet place in the woods I would be free to think and write again.

The mirror-image room across the hall had windows that were exposed to southern light. For a time, we dedicated that space as Toni's studio. To be at Little Creek meant a new beginning for her art, just as it was for my writing. There were new techniques with oils and pastels for her to explore, a new nature to observe, new landscapes to paint.

Ever since I was a child, my preference has been to be out of doors where there are no walls to confine me or ceilings to block my view of the sky. Although the inside of the cabin provided a welcoming environment, I favored the openness of the porch

SHELTER

that spanned the building's front and afforded a view of both ponds and the woods beyond. The veranda's floor was made of treated planks. Two paddle fans were installed to circulate the air on warm summer days. A double swing hung from the ceiling by chains. We sat there by the hour, gently moving back and forth to the slow rhythm of our life while observing the birds that visited our feeders or a butterfly milking nectar from a flower.

The porch's rustic furnishings included two old rockers with seats of woven cane strips and a brass coffee table that had been in Toni's family. A long wooden picnic table with bench seats that accommodated eight comfortably was where we enjoyed most of our meals alfresco. Occasionally, we entertained our friends there at small candlelit dinners. There was a cherry chest where we stowed bug spray and toys for Toni's grandchildren and eventually mine. On a copper tray by the door, we lined up our footwear—a pair of Wellington boots, Crocs, hiking boots, and running shoes. We carved wooden walking sticks, lacquered them with polyurethane, and hung them by leather thongs where they were handy when needed for hikes through the woods. At an antique mall in nearby Edinburgh, we purchased an old iron ship's bell that I attached to a post. In the evening, Toni often rang the bell to summon me from the woods for a drink. The metallic clang echoing through the valley was like the sound of an Angelus bell sanctifying the day.

Perry Olds's wife, Irene Joslin, is a musician and vocalist who sang blues and jazz with a band called the Amalgamators at the Fig Tree, a coffeehouse in nearby Helmsburg. At one end of the porch, Perry had constructed an open wooden deck where, on summer evenings, the Amalgamators played while people danced on the porch. I have been told their parties were hoedowns, legendary in their excesses. The guests built bonfires, pitched tents on the dam, swilled beer and wine, and partied through the night. There was a time when Toni and I would have enjoyed these raucous affairs. Our lifestyle, however, befitting our age, had simplified and quieted. Our taste in music had metamorphosed from rock to classical and jazz. We used the deck as a place for a steamer chair where, as if on a luxury liner, I could lounge and read in the afternoon with the tops of maple trees lapping around me like waves.

SHELTER

After a summer of getting to know Little Creek and what our needs were, we found our quarters cramped when family or guests stayed overnight. Also, Toni needed a larger studio and I a study with shelves for my books. The solution was to remodel the barn loft into a guest room and artist's studio. Toni's old studio in the cabin then could become my study.

I knew of one builder I wanted for the work. He was Rick Ryan, a master craftsman who had done remodeling projects for me in the past. My concern, however, was Rick's health. He had been diagnosed with leukemia and was recovering from chemotherapy and a bone marrow transplant. When I called him, I was pleased to learn he wanted the work and was well enough to take it on.

Rick drove to Little Creek in a big van with two hundred thousand miles on the odometer and lumber and tools in the back. He looked like a mountain man. He wore heavy canvas pants with a rip in the knee, an old gray T-shirt that showed his thick arms, and a sweat-stained felt cowboy hat to cover his shaved head. His chest-length beard was always matted with sawdust, his glasses smudged. His appearance frightened Oscar, and the terrier barked at him continually. Rick retaliated by calling the neutered dog a "dud stud."

With a thermos of coffee and bottles of Powerade to keep him going, Rick worked ten to twelve hours a day, taking a short break at noon when he ate a banana and a granola bar and washed down a handful of pain pills with water. I worried about him and his bone marrow. His platelet count was low. When he cut himself, he wouldn't stop bleeding until I applied a pressure dressing. I wondered if his leukemia was relapsing. But I believe one's medical issues are privileged information. I wasn't his doctor, and I didn't talk to him about his illness unless he asked me a direct question. When he did, I could tell he was concerned about his longevity. How could he not be? Although he wasn't knowledgeable about granulocytes, erythrocytes, and megakaryocytes, Rick was smart. He understood as well as I did that healthy blood cells are critical to life. Some nights he stayed with us so he wouldn't have to waste time and gas on the forty-mile trip back to his farmhouse in Scipio. On those occasions, he brought deer sausage for an appetizer and thick T-bone steaks from a cow he had butchered. Toni added baked potatoes and a salad. He was divorced, and I think to be with us allayed his loneliness and guilt, something I could relate to.

To find where the sewer and water lines were buried, Rick used the ancient technique of dowsing, or water witching. In his hand, he loosely held a divining rod made of a twenty-inch length of fence wire bent in an "L." With its tip slightly below the horizontal, he asked the rod to find the energy emitted from the water beneath the earth. I was skeptical, but soon the rod began to swing gently from side to side until it aligned itself with the water lines. He let me try it. I swear it worked for me, too. Rick marked on the ground with spray paint where the rod led him. When he dug, he was right on the water.

The studio's steps he built with a short rise and a pipe railing to make it easy for us old folks to climb. Outside the entry to the loft, Rick constructed a second-story deck, twelve feet by twelve feet. The structure overlooked a deep wooded ravine where black snakes slithered among the bloodroot and whitetails bounded over fallen beeches. Airy and elemental, the view was poetry and religion. Often before entering the building, I lingered at the railing in a moment of awe and contemplation.

In one corner of the loft, Rick built a small bathroom. He installed a shower and our splurge, a vanity with a marble top. He created a partition to separate the sleeping area, where there was room for twin beds and Mother's antique walnut chest of drawers. We nestled a kitchenette beside the bathroom. The stainless-steel sink was for Toni to wash her paintbrushes. We repurposed cherry-wood cabinets from the cabin and added a small refrigerator, where we stored wine and water for guests.

All day long, the clank of Rick's hammer and the zing of his saw sang through the hills. Fatigue showed on his face, but he kept going. He seemed powered and sustained by an energy and determination that came with a passion for his work and, I imagine, a fear of time's limits. I believe I approached surgery in the same way. Now I must seek other passions and not cling to the past.

In my new study, Rick installed pine shelves he had fashioned in his workshop. They were to hold the books I had rescued from the house in Columbus. The cabin was out of plumb, making it difficult to level the shelves. But Rick made it work with shims and trim. With a roller, I helped him paint the walls a pale shade of sage. I liked working with Rick. I relished learning from him about plumbing and heating, wiring and carpentry, goat farming and deer hunting. He knew nature— trees, birds, fish, and plants—from a hunter's point of view. We didn't talk sports or politics because he didn't care about them, but he did acknowledge he liked Obama, although he was afraid the young president would take his guns away. I didn't tell him I wished he would.

The tasks Rick gave me required little skill, only a willingness to sweat. Even so, Rick was a meticulous taskmaster and insisted I do everything right. It reminded me of the way I had demanded the team in an operating room perform. Now I dug a drainage trench. I spread creek gravel with a bucket and shovel. I wore a surgical mask and safety glasses when I insulated the garage ceiling with fiberglass. My old muscles quivered as I strained to hold sheets of corrugated metal while Rick screwed them to beams with a power drill. There was something about manual labor that made me feel authentic, even dignified.

A surgeon leaves traces of himself on the patients he operates upon. I can tell something about the doctor, his ability and knowledge and what kind of a person he was, when I see the size and location of the incision he used or the scars he left behind. A builder also leaves traces of himself in what he builds. I think when someone comes along years from now and sees the craftsmanship of the loft, the mitered corners and Rick's finishing touches, whoever it is will know the builder was talented and hard-working, honest in what he did. A man who took no shortcuts.

When Rick finished, we celebrated by inviting him and his grown son and daughter, Jason and Sierra, for dinner so his children could see what their father had accomplished. As we toured the new studio, I told them they should be proud of their daddy. Sierra and Jason said they were.

The day of moving into the new studio and study, we awakened early like children on Christmas morning. After a quick cup of coffee, we hurried to the loft. I helped Toni set up a big wooden easel. She laid out her paints on a worktable made from a door and placed her brushes in jars. She hooked up her iPod and hung her watercolor botanicals and oil Brown County landscapes by clothespins from a wire on the wall. On a small table in a corner of the room, she laid out a sumi painting set she had purchased for me when we visited the Metropolitan Museum in New York to see the

SHELTER

Chinese garden. She hoped I would enjoy the art of Japanese brush painting. Although I was short on artistic ability, I was anxious to give it a try. Toni placed her art books on a stepladder shelf and stowed her canvasses in a closet. From her easel, she hung a white lab coat I had worn when seeing patients in the office. It pleased me to know it would now be her artist's smock.

In my study, under the window, Rick and I positioned another door on top of two filing cabinets to make a desk where I could write in a quiet, well-lighted place. On the cherry floor, I spread a small oriental rug I had bought in a shop on the Left Bank in Paris when my daughter, Katie, now a French teacher, was a student there. I loved Paris. I had been there many times and wanted to go back. In recent years, travel had become somewhat taxing for Toni and me. Sometimes I felt as if Little Creek marked the end of a long journey. But I knew it was too soon to stop exploring new places, too soon to stop seeking new ideas.

Nothing makes a room more beautiful than books, floor to ceiling. To me, a home without them is like a person missing a mind or heart. Thoreau had written, "Books are the treasured wealth of the world and the fit inheritance of generations and nations. Books, the oldest and the best stand naturally and rightfully on the shelves of every cottage." It pleased me to know Thoreau would approve of my cottage.

It took a couple of days for me to unpack boxes and shelve all of my volumes. I considered my books among my wisest and most dependable friends. To be reunited with them was delightful. Often I paused to read a paragraph or two from the work of a favorite author, such as James Salter's *Light Years* or Raymond Carver's *Where I'm Calling From*. I set aside a shelf for poetry, one for philosophy and religion, other shelves for medical texts, history, and biography, and many for my collection of literary fiction. There was a section for my own publications and one for the books of my writer friends: Sena Naslund and Lucinda Dixon Sullivan from Louisville; Barb Shoup, Vesle Fenstermaker, and Nancy Kriplen from Indianapolis; Tom McGuane, Jane Geniesse, and Alice Gorman from Florida; Lou Ann Walker, Speed Vogel, and Joe Heller from New York. I placed Thoreau's *Walden* and Wendell Berry's *The Long-Legged House* on the desk because I referred to them frequently. They were guidebooks to an elemental life. On the back wall, I displayed my diplomas, as doctors with egos tend to

SHELTER

do. But it seemed okay to take a bow. As Toni reminded me, I had saved a life or two.

That evening Toni I toasted each other with a glass of wine on the studio's deck. The evening was magnificent, cool with clear air, the trees filled with light. High above, a red-tailed hawk cried and soared on spread wings, its benediction to the end of day. I saw the contrail of a jet en route to somewhere we didn't want to go. I was content for the moment to be where I was, at Little Creek. I probably paid too much for the property and spent more on the remodeling than I should have, but to me, the cabin and barn were priceless. I was grateful to have my health and to be free to be myself, grateful to be living with Toni in such a peaceful and rustic place sheltered by sturdy logs. A home warm with affections.

Touch the earth, love the earth, honor the earth,
her plains, her valleys, her hills, and her seas,
rest your spirit in her solitary places.

ERNEST DIMNET

EARTH

When Toni and I arrived at Little Creek in May of 2009, the white dogwoods were in bloom and so were the irises, or blue flags as my grandmother, Mamma Bess, called them. Red-petaled columbine and purple violets provided their nectar to butterflies and bumblebees. Bloodroots were popping up in the woods. Seedlings with a metallic sheen were everywhere. Mushrooms poked their red, blue, and yellow helmets through clumps of green ferns. All the plants were flowering earlier in the season than they once did when the earth was cooler and the Miami Indians roamed the Brown County hills searching for game. This manifestation of climate change gave me pause. I tried to imagine what the planet would be like when my grandchildren were my age. Where will the glaciers be? The ice flows? The shores?

The leaves of the oaks and maples that surround the cabin emerged, green and tender, replicating their pattern of last year and the years before. The ponds were full to the brim with water from winter snows and spring rains. New blades of wild grass bent with the wind. The sky shone fresh and blue. It was a time when the future seemed somewhat less distant, the past less daunting. I wanted to be outside in the open air, to be in contact with the soil, to smell the earth and touch it.

I am not a farmer. The closest I came to tilling the soil was when I was a small boy during the war, helping my father weed his Victory Garden in the field behind his funeral home. I can vaguely remember the sweet corn and tomatoes he raised and the pride he displayed when his produce appeared on Mother's table. But in spite of my urbanized upbringing, I have the instincts of a farmer. I can feel the magnetic pull of the earth. If I were seeking an elemental life in the near wilderness, it seemed only right that I should give in to the land's gravitational force and plant gardens.

On a Tuesday morning after a spring shower had passed through and softened the earth, I went on a planting frenzy. I broadcast a blend of mail-order wildflower seeds onto a grassy slope. I filled terra cotta pots with pink impatiens and arranged them on a shady deck. With a spade, I heaved up irises and day lilies, divided them, and planted them in new locations in the perennial gardens surrounding the cabin's entryway. Then I added a few peony bushes and marigolds to the mix of coneflowers and black-eyed Susans. The sun on my shoulders and back soothed me. As a surgeon, clean hands and fingernails were imperative. Now my hands were dirty, and I didn't care.

The following morning when the grass was still wet, I went to the woods and dug up ferns and myrtle to line the steps I had built from the cabin to the pond. I worked quietly in the sunshine, hacking out a hole for a fern with a pickax. Suddenly, I heard a scream coming from somewhere in the forest to the east of the pond. It was a human sound, high pitched and full of terror and pain. Startled, I dropped my pick. Half afraid of what I might find, I hurried down to the shore. Had someone been hurt? We were miles from anyone. Who could it be? What I saw was the head of a deer moving toward me in the water. The doe's eyes were wide and black. She labored, swimming as fast as her thin legs would take her. A wedge of ripples followed her in the dark water. I wondered if she would drown. I thought if she went under, I would swim to her and try to pull her out of the water. I was relieved when she reached the dam. The little deer struggled out of the pond and dashed into the woods. She was young, small-boned and lithe with a fawn's spotted coat. In a few seconds, I heard a splash and saw her again, swimming in the lower pond. I wondered what was she fleeing. A coyote? A poacher? Nature's savagery and uncertainties seemed close at hand.

EARTH

For most of my life, I had considered the earth a place created for man to live on and use as he saw fit. My short time at Little Creek, however, caused me to realize that like the little doe, I was just one form of life among many other forms of life. The deer and I were both here on earth at God's pleasure and mercy. As Archibald MacLeish wrote so eloquently, "To see the earth as it truly is, small and blue and beautiful in that eternal silence where it floats, is to see ourselves as riders on the earth together, brothers on that bright loveliness in the eternal cold."

A century ago, Brown County was a harbinger of what is happening to the earth today. People began to recklessly clear cut its hillsides. They carted the lumber to Indianapolis for railroad ties, barrel staves, hoop poles, and furniture. After the land was treeless, county residents tried to plant wheat and corn where the hardwood once grew. However, by 1900 erosion had washed the topsoil from the hillsides. Nothing could grow. Poverty ensued. The county's population dropped from ten thousand to five thousand in 1930. Deserted cabins stood everywhere in the county's deeply carved valleys and on its high ridges. It took fifty years for reforested trees to grow back. Only then did people and their spirit return to Brown County.

With that history in mind, I was determined to be a good steward of the land and intrude as little as possible on the environment. Therefore, I chose for my vegetable garden a narrow strip of land at the foot of a hill behind the cabin that had already been cleared. The plot received full sunlight, and the cabin's hose could reach it for irrigation. Also, since it was elevated on a terrace with a wall of railroad ties, I could weed it without bending over and straining my tender old back.

One afternoon bright with sunlight, Toni and I drove a few miles north of Bean Blossom to a small backyard nursery in the village of Fruitdale. Strolling through rows of wet green shrubs, flowers, and seedling trees, I wanted to buy everything and plant it. The owner, a ruddy-faced country woman, was an artist who had painted a Monet-like mural of water lilies on the side of her barn. She was chatty and friendly and knew her plant material well. She advised me on what liked shade and what liked sun. She picked out the healthiest specimens and carted them to the car in a child's red wagon. She said she didn't trust credit cards, so I paid her in cash.

EARTH

From my builder friend, Rick Ryan, I borrowed a rototiller to turn the earth. The machine strained as its blades cut into the dense and pasty red clay. The soil appeared to be tired and infertile. With a rake, I mixed in several fifty-pound sacks of garden soil and peat to make it loamy. A dark, boggy odor wafted from the enriched earth. I planted mint, oregano, basil, parsley, chives, and thyme, then three tomato plants—Cherry Grandes, Romas, and Wonder Boys. With a trowel, I scooped out pockets in the dirt for acorn squash and zucchini, peppers and onions. A line for one of my haikus came to me —"In the garden I am alone but never lonely."

I am a carnivore. Toni, once a vegan, is a devotee of green vegetables. She relishes asparagus, broccoli, Brussels spouts, arugula, and spinach. She would hope that Thoreau was right when he wrote, "I have no doubt that it is a part of the destiny of the human race, in its gradual improvement, to leave off eating animals, as surely as the savage tribes have left off eating each other." In deference to her civilized taste for that which is leafy and green, I planted a small patch of Swiss chard and leaf lettuce.

At times in my life, I have defined myself in various ways—student, ball player, soldier, husband, father, writer, doctor—especially doctor. Alone in the wilderness working the soil with a spade, it was as if I were being redefined. I felt like a stranger to my past, someone nobody but Toni knew. The important question was, however: Did I know myself?

When the garden was in the ground, I gave the plants and seeds a thorough soaking with water pumped from the pond. Tired and sweaty, I rinsed the mud from my hands. For a while, I sat on a nearby bench and gazed at the garden. I knew the small crop of vegetables and herbs wouldn't impact our nutrition or save us money. It wouldn't help feed the hungry. But nonetheless, a sense of accomplishment washed over me. The tendrils of the plant's roots seemed to attach me to the earth.

As summer passed, the plants struggled to survive. I knew that even with the addition of a soil supplement, the earth at Little Creek wasn't rich enough to grow a bountiful crop. Next year I wanted to provide the clay soil with more carbon, nitrogen, phosphorus, and potassium. But I didn't want to pollute the land and water with chemicals and manufactured fertilizer. I decided to do it organically.

EARTH

Bloomingfoods is a co-op thirty miles away in Bloomington, Indiana. It sells locally grown and naturally produced foods as well as seed and gardening supplies. I read in the newspaper that the co-op was sponsoring a half-price sale of the Earth Machine home composter. *Perfect,* I thought, *an Earth Machine.* It sounded supernatural, like a time machine.

Early on a Saturday morning, I drove to the town where my father had attended Indiana University seventy-seven years ago. West of Nashville, the state park's fifteen thousand acres was still under the gaze of a pale moon. Dense fog layered in its hollows like smoke. Seeing the vast unspoiled wilderness gave me hope.

At the co-op, I waited in a long line of women with babies in backpacks like papooses and lean, bearded men wearing T-shirts, cargo shorts, and Birkenstocks. They obviously were tree huggers, a designation I once considered derogatory. Standing there in line with them, I realized I had become one of them.

The round Earth Machine measured three feet high and three feet in diameter with a capacity of ten cubic feet. It was made of recycled polyethylene and painted black to retain heat. A slotted lid allowed oxygen into the compost. I bought one for fifty dollars. Under the stairway to the loft, I screwed the composter to the ground with twist pegs. I circled its base with a layer of bricks to keep out burrowing critters and Oscar. Beside the kitchen sink, Toni placed a metal canister with a tight, rubber-sealed top where we stored our food scraps—eggshells, coffee grounds, leftover bread and pasta, spoils of fruits and vegetables, but not meat or dairy products. When the canister was full, I transferred its contents to the Earth Machine. Once a week, I wet down the pile and stirred it with a metal rod to allow oxygen into the mix and encourage the growth of bacteria and fungi. The decay smelled sweet, like fermenting grapes. Occasionally, I threw in a few earthworms to digest and mix the organic material. I kept the compost covered with a layer of carbon-rich leaves, dead flowers, and yard debris to hold down the fruit fly population. Why was I going to all this trouble to produce a meager eighty gallons of compost a year? The answer is because I believe man and his appetites are destroying this beautiful, blue earth we ride on. I wanted to help extend that ride and keep it beautiful and blue even in my meager way.

During the hot days of August and September, Toni and I kept the garden wa-

EARTH

tered and weeded, but the harvest was modest. The herbs did well. Our salads and sauces were flavorful with cuttings of sweet-scented basil and oregano. Mint spiced our iced tea. Parsley garnished our plates. A single zucchini made its appearance in Toni's skillet sprinkled with salt and pepper and sautéed in olive oil. With enough parmesan cheese added, it wasn't bad. The green peppers were stunted but added zest to my spaghetti sauce. There was enough leaf lettuce for an occasional salad of mixed greens tossed with my own vinaigrette dressing. The tomatoes were our most successful crop. Toni served them in a variety of ways: grilled with bread crumbs, sliced with mozzarella cheese, basil, and olive oil, speared as kabobs, and as an appetizer marinated with vodka. But nothing tasted better than picking a ripe red tomato from the vine and eating it with plenty of salt while the fruit was still warm.

I'm sorry to report the Swiss chard was a failure. The few leaves that broke ground were small and pale. Even the rabbits ignored them. Toni accused me of spraying the plants with growth retardant. A squirrel ate the lone acorn squash. No trace of an onion was ever seen.

The true harvest of our garden, however, wasn't something we could eat. It was something that fed my soul.

I believe a leaf of grass is no less than
the journey-work of the stars.

WALT WHITMAN

LIGHT

In high school and college physics, I studied optics and electricity, as well as the properties of light, the electromagnetic spectrum, and the atomic numbers of the elements. In medical school, I studied the eye, its rods and cones, its vitreous and choroid plexus. I once built a Tesla coil that emitted high-frequency waves that could light a bulb in the next room. Experiments taught me the characteristics of light but not its nature.

Just as certain birds are my favorites to watch on the Little Creek property, so are occurrences of light. In early morning the green iridescence of a sunlit patch of wild grass by the pond is particularly pleasing to my eyes. The light that shines on the yellow petals of black-eyed Susans and buttercups brightens my afternoons. I never tire of watching the silver shimmer of evening light as it plays on the ripples of the pond when fish are feeding. These displays of light exert power over me and elevate my mood.

Vincent van Gogh thought that the night was more alive and more richly colored than the day. Nights at Little Creek are illuminated by a variety of lights that seem to bear him out. After dark, fireflies wink endlessly in the valley below the porch. Like strobe lights at a disco, the twinkling scene is about courtship. The males are trying to woo the females by blinking their cool yellow posteriors. The females signal consent by a flash of their taillights.

When I watch these photoelectric bugs, I am a boy again in a meadow with my sister. It is the summer of 1948. Sandra and I are capturing lightning bugs and putting them in a mayonnaise jar with holes in the lid. Carefree, it didn't occur to me that things could change and die. But things did change, abruptly and dramatically.

The following day Mother drove me in her Buick to the city park where I was to play baseball. The sun boiled down. Heat rose from the pavement. Wavy images made it appear as if I were looking through a glass bottle. When I stepped up to bat, I felt woozy. My head throbbed. My neck was stiff. The light hurt my eyes, and I closed them. I didn't see the ball coming at me. I vomited and crumbled to the ground. It was polio. I spent the summer in Ball Memorial Hospital in Muncie unable to eat, at times near death. My throat and palate were paralyzed. When I was finally able to come home, Mother blenderized my food and fed it to me through a tube she inserted into my stomach. I eventually recovered with little residual paralysis except for a nasal voice and difficulty swallowing. I think polio led me to medicine. I don't remember collecting lightning bugs again, but surely I did.

When friends come to the cabin for dinner, Toni lines the railing of the porch with candles in glass jars. She lights the table with two kerosene lanterns and more candles. The porch becomes a grotto. Solar lights line the driveway and show our guests the way. I see their orange glow and contemplate the mysteries of light. Where did it come from? What is light? Waves or quantums? How can it be stored? Where does light go in darkness?

One artificial light inside the cabin has particular significance. On my parents' twenty-fifth wedding anniversary, my father took Mother to Ireland. It was a way of paying homage to her Irish heritage. Mother loved things that sparkle. At the Waterford factory in Dublin, she purchased a crystal chandelier. It was a beautiful jewel of a light fixture with pendants and prisms. She hung it above her dining room table, where for years it illuminated Christmas and Thanksgiving dinners. The same chandelier also illuminated the hospital bed that replaced the dining table when I came home from the hospital after polio. It was there under the prisms Mother fed me through a tube.

After Mother died, the chandelier became mine. I had no place to hang it, so I considered selling it. But when Toni saw it, she said it would make an eclectic decoration in our rustic cottage. I thought the idea might be a little over the top, but I trusted her taste. The light was hung above a worn oak table and four flea-market chairs in the corner of the main room. The mirror behind it reflects the glitter from droplets of glass. The chandelier's flame-shaped bulbs radiate more than visible waves of energy. They radiate waves of memories and deep affections.

As the light of Provence enticed van Gogh, Cezanne, and Picasso to southern France, the light of Brown County has attracted many artists to southern Indiana to paint its landscapes. In the late 1800s, T. C. Steele, Marie Goth, Carl Graf, V. J. Cariani, and other fine American impressionists migrated to Brown County and adopted it as their home and muse. A thriving colony of Hoosier artists still exists in the county. Their studios are everywhere in the hills. Toni's at Little Creek is among them.

Toni is a connoisseur of light. She knows its flavors, the behavior and nuances of its rays. She knows the moods of light and how to evoke them with paint applied to a canvas. Once I asked her to tell me something about light and painting. She simply said, "Painting is an interpretation of light."

In the barn's loft, abundant light bathes Toni's studio. The walls are paneled in beadboard painted white to reflect and maximize luminescence. At one end of the room, tall French doors admit the same northerly light that Leonardo de Vinci said was the best for drawing. At the other end, the loft's loading door has been converted into a large mullioned window that overlooks the cabin and the pond. Two skylights in the roof above Toni's easel let in southeasterly light. Exposed rafters of the high open ceiling are lined with florescent bulbs that allow the light to remain constant throughout the day.

Every afternoon, I visit Toni in her studio. I like to see what she is painting, like to see her wearing my white doctor's coat as a smock. Oscar sleeps at her side on his

LIGHT

denim bed. Some days an opera plays on the radio. Often the air is pungent with the scent of burning incense. Like all true artists, Toni comes to the world with a different way of seeing. She can take something as simple as a squash blossom and create an image in watercolor that is both simple and complex. It is as if she is able to look into the plant's soul. To paraphrase what was once said of Cezanne's painting: "Each stroke of [her] brush contains the air, the light, the object, the composition, the character, the outline, and [her] style." Her studio is a magical place for me to be.

I often drive Toni around the Indiana countryside, searching for new landscapes with proper light for her to photograph and then paint. One bright summer morning, we began our odyssey with a visit to my ninety-five-year-old father. Daddy was living in an extended-care facility in Muncie, Indiana, named Morrison Woods. There were no trees on the property. It is ironic Toni and I started a quest for light there because my father was legally blind from macular degeneration. All he saw were shadows and shades of gray. What he did see he could barely comprehend. When I looked at his watery, red eyes with the lower lids everted and inflamed, I felt sad for him. Macular degeneration may be inherited. Was I standing on the threshold of blindness? Darkness is where we begin and where we end.

From Muncie, Toni and I drove east to Farmland. The rural village was eight miles from Winchester, the small county seat where I grew up. When I was a college student on a summer job, I painted a house in Farmland that was the office of the Eastern Indiana Telephone Company. It was a picturesque village then with red geraniums in window boxes and clotheslines where Monday's wash dried in the sun. I hoped there would be something in the town, a house or garden, that would catch Toni's eye and inspire her to paint it. But Farmland had changed. The town had become "artsy-fartsy," as my dad would have said when he still had a wit about him. What had once seemed quaint was merely contrived. Gone was the hardware store where I purchased turpentine, drop cloths, and paintbrushes. The corner cafe where I ate chicken-fried steak at a counter, elbow to elbow with farmhands, was now an ice cream parlor that sold walnut fudge and gourmet popcorn. Nothing struck me as authentic. Toni saw nothing to paint.

LIGHT

Disappointed, we left the town and headed south on State Road 1 through the rolling terrain of eastern Indiana. The two-lane blacktop meandered along a stream the color of slate. Splendid open fields of corn and soybeans flowed by, all washed in sunlight as yellow as the rind of a lemon. I stopped while Toni snapped pictures of a red barn and an ancient dog asleep under a chestnut oak. An old man wearing overalls and a curled straw hat stood on a porch considering the sky. I peered through the windshield to see what he was seeing. In the light of late morning, the sky was periwinkle, the clouds feathery and high.

We continued through the tiny crossroad settlement of Losantville, where several residents claim to have seen ghosts. Further on was Modoc and Huntsville, where I had played high school basketball in barn-like gyms. Our team was the Yellow Jackets. Cheerleaders with pompoms and good legs urged us on. "Sting 'em Yellow Jackets. Sting 'em." I tried to explain "Hoosier Hysteria" to Toni. I told her I had been a part of something mythic.

"Something mythic?" she said. "Or a myth?"

"Mythic," I said.

Wonderful pastoral settings blanketed both sides of the road. The landscape was plain, unadorned middle America. Periodically, I pulled onto the shoulder. Through an open window, Toni photographed what caught her eye: lavender thistles in a ditch, cornstalks at close range all gold and green in a fever-yellow light. A herd of spotted Herefords waded in a pond, their reflection blurred in muddy water. A white farmhouse stood stark and isolated as if waiting to be painted by Edward Hopper. The silver silos of a grain elevator jutted into the sky like the pipes of an organ. I stopped at a railroad crossing while Toni snapped a shot of rusty train tracks that seemed to lead straight to eternity, as in another Hopper painting, *House by the Railroad*. A woman in curlers and an apron hung her laundry out to dry. She waved as we passed by. There was gentleness about the land and the people. Toni and my time together seemed timeless. Late in the afternoon, we turned our faces toward the setting sun and headed west, back to Brown County.

One night after a long day of lifting stones to build a wall, I trudged up the stairs

LIGHT

to the bedroom. I was tired and looking forward to sleep. A splendid pale light filled the room. I went to the window and looked out. The moon shone full and large. Its mirror image shimmered on the pond. It was a lovely sight, that reflection of the moon on dark water. I thought of Neil Armstrong, the first man to walk on the lunar surface. I had the honor of knowing Neil through Roger Howe, a friend in Florida. Neil was a brilliant but humble man. I consider him the most heroic of American heroes. There at the bedroom window, I pictured the earth as it must have appeared through Neil's eyes, small and glowing and insignificant. I turned my gaze to the stars. I saw the Big Dipper, Orion's Belt, and the Milky Way, all millions of light years away. Even though the stars may have burned out, their light lingered.

I am fire and air, my other elements I give to baser life.

WILLIAM SHAKESPEARE
Antony and Cleopatra, Act V

AIR

I love the air at Little Creek. It flows through the property on prevailing westerly winds. Crystalline and pure, it allows all you see to be sharply defined. The Brown County atmosphere is pristine because it is relatively unpolluted by the smoky wastes and toxic exhausts of man's chimneys and pipes. Also, the hardwood forests of Brown County State Park, the Hoosier National Forest, and Yellowwood State Forest occupy a majority of the county's acreage. These trees are the lungs of the land. Millions of leaves cleanse the atmosphere. They remove carbon dioxide, sulfur dioxide, ozone and microparticles through their stomata and pour oxygen back into the air.

Much like unpolluted water is to marine life, this fresh cleansed air of Little Creek is a perfect biosphere for not only human life but avian life, too. I am amazed at the number of birds that live on the property. Different species are everywhere. They ride high above on thermal currents, nest under the porch's eave, swim on the ponds, perch in the trees, call to us night and day.

Although I was a zoology major as well as a pre-med student in college, I always seemed to be too busy to observe birds in their own environment. I saw them, but I really didn't see them. I knew something of bird anatomy and physiology, how their wings were airfoils that lifted them by Bernoulli's principle, how they were members of the phylum *Chordata,* how their lungs were little air sacs called alveoli, and that their brains were small. But other than their science, I knew little else about birds. My being too precise and scientific about flora and fauna diminished my appreciation of them. As the Buddha said, "If you think too much, you miss the flower." Part of the transformation I wanted to make in Little Creek's wilderness was to gear myself down and take the time to observe and appreciate nature more deeply.

In *Walden,* Thoreau quoted the "Harivansa," a poem of Yoga philosophy. The verse said, "An abode without birds is like a meat without seasoning." To season our lives, one of the first things Toni and I did after settling into our log cabin was to begin feeding the birds. This commitment turned out to be time consuming and somewhat expensive. It required binoculars, bird books, feeders, and forty-pound bags of seed that we stored in the barn in metal cans with tight lids to keep the rodents out. In spite of my aversion to constant communication with humanity, I own an iPhone. On it, I downloaded the iBird Explorer Plus app. This bird-watcher's field guide has an inventory of 941 species of North American birds. One touch of the phone's screen, and I can summon a reference to the bird I spied. I can also talk to it by playing its call. One wonders if Thoreau would approve.

From the eave of the porch, we hung two Droll Yankee tube feeders and a sixteen-ounce hummingbird feeder. Toni made the hummingbird's liquid diet by dissolving one part sugar in four parts of water. I filled one feeder on the overhang with a mix of hulled sunflower seeds, niger seed, millet, and black-oil sunflower seeds. The other we stocked with thistle.

On mornings when the air was fresh with anticipation and the pond shone like a dark eye, we sat in the porch swing to enjoy a cup of coffee. There is no newspaper delivery at Little Creek. The day begins with a bird serenade, not a barrage of troublesome news about wars and deceptions.

We soon learned that there was a pecking order at the feeders. The black-capped chickadees arrived first to take advantage of pre-dawn light and extend their foraging time. Chickadees, feathered in black and gray, are drab, but we found their dour appearance was deceiving. The little birds were cheerful, non-combative, and acrobatic. They hung upside-down while they pecked at seeds in the feeder. It confounded me that chickadees don't migrate. How could a bird so small survive winter when nature's shelves were nearly empty? My research taught me that evolution had selected for chicks those that were able to replace their summer plumage with warmer winter feathers as well as for the ones that were able to lower their body temperature at night and enter a state of hypothermia. This semi-hibernation reduced their fat consumption and lessened their need for food.

Nuthatches, chickadees, and their cousins, the titmice, were messy eaters. Spilled seeds covered the ground under the feeders and attracted doves. These soft gray and beige birds collected the seeds and stored them in their crop, a pouch in the esophagus. Later both the males and females would feed their chicks crop milk, a gruel from these partially digested seeds. The doves "coo coo coo" sounded like a lament. I can't look at a dove without remembering when a friend of my dad's, an avid bird hunter, brought us several doves he had shot. No wonder the lament. Mother reluctantly cooked them. They tasted terrible to me, all bones and buckshot.

It took a while for the finches to get up courage to come to the feeder, but when they arrived, they stole the show. Singing and scolding, these passerine birds flitted and fought. At times we had six goldfinches vying for a spot on a perch. Self-important and domineering, the males were dressed a brilliant shade of yellow. The females were the color of week-old bananas but just as feisty.

The story of the finch's beak is the best-known story of survival of the fittest. It was first told by Charles Darwin in his *Voyage of the Beagle,* then documented by evolutionary biologists Peter and Rosemary Grant. Their research was a transcendent work of natural history. Suffice it to say, the Grants found that different food sources predicted different shapes of the finch's bills.

The beaks of the finches at Little Creek were strong and stubby. I watched them peck at the thistle and wondered what the characteristics of their bills would be in the years to come. The story of evolution told me it all depended on what would be left for them to eat in an ever-warming world.

AIR

The cardinal was one of the few birds I could identify by its song. On summer mornings a cardinal's slow trill called me from my bed—"cheer, cheer, cheer, what, what, what." These beautiful scarlet birds tended to keep to themselves. It pleased me when they appeared at the feeders. The male of the species was a regal, brilliant red with a crested head. He wore a black face mask, as if going to a costume ball as the Lone Ranger. The female's feathers were greenish like old copper. Her mate was a willing provider. He plucked a sunflower seed from the feeder, cracked it in his beak, then passed the meat of the seed to his mate. This little act of sharing with his partner touched me. It seemed like the epitome of love. The next time we had pistachios, I cracked one for Toni.

I wondered why the male cardinal was permitted to wear his bright red coat of feathers. Wouldn't its vividness attract predators such as owls and hawks and threaten the survival of his species? I found the answer, where else but on the internet. Studies showed that a raptor's perception of colors differs from that of humans. What's bright to them is dull to us, and the reverse is true. Also I learned that brighter red males rule over larger territories with denser vegetation. This allows them to feed at higher rates and have greater reproductive success. What did the blues singer John Lee Hooker Jr. suggest?

Put on your red dress baby
And let me one more time
Make you smile tonight.

My study of ruby-throated hummingbirds was like watching magicians perform tricks. The acrobatics of these tiny creatures looked impossible. They hovered near the sugar water feeder or flew backwards, maneuvering like a helicopter. These birds' hearts beat six hundred times per minute, their wings seventy times per second, humming as the bird's name suggests. They were little metabolic machines. They burned calories fifty times faster than I did. This required replenishing their carbohydrate supply every fifteen minutes. When they left the feeder, I knew they would be back before long, needling their beaks into the cylinder of sweet water. Of course these characteristics were due to evolution, not accident. The curve and length of the beaks of the different species of hummingbirds conformed to the anatomy of the flowers that supplied their nectar. The ability to hover evolved because the flowers that fed them had no place for the birds to perch.

The feeding station dramas absorbed me. It was like entering a little paradise. But I couldn't help wonder if in feeding the birds I was actually doing harm. In the way conservatives argue against the welfare state, I didn't want a flock of lazy and dependent birds on my hands. Nor did I wish to drive them in a new evolutionary direction. But where was the balance? I continue to feed the birds and ponder the question.

My favorite bird on the property was one that didn't visit the feeders. It was the barred owl that nested somewhere in the dense foliage near the driveway. "Emperor of the Air," I called him. The owl often greeted us on our arrival home by flying low over the road in front of the car, then peeling off into the trees. It glided on wings that spanned at least three feet. Dark eyed and yellow beaked, he received his name from the striped plumage on his chest and belly. Like most owls, he was a nocturnal animal. Some nights I heard him calling, "hoo, hoo, two hoo." If no one was around to hear me, I called back, "who cooks for you, who cooks for you all." This bird intrigued me because it was serious and aloof, a self-sufficient loner. But he wasn't above accepting handouts. When I trapped a mouse in the barn or the pantry, I placed the dead rodent on the side of the road near where I thought the owl's nest might be. The offering was usually gone the next day.

As I have done for over thirty years, I jogged each morning. At Little Creek my route was an undulating stretch of gravel road that led from the barn to the cairn that marked the entry to the property. I made a round-trip three times, covering about two miles in thirty minutes, a box turtle's pace but fast enough to get my heart rate up and keep my weight down and my cardiovascular system fit. It was a chance to breathe the clean air of Little Creek, full of oxygen from the trees and free of acid rain. If I was lucky along the way, I encountered a flock of twelve wild turkeys, a hen and her brood of maturing chicks. The turkeys nested nearby in the vines and brush of an opening in the woods. As omnivores, they foraged for acorns, seeds, and salamanders. With their fleshy wattles, the turkeys were rather homely but venerable. They fanned their chestnut-brown tail feathers and strutted. They recalled another era, a time when Indians lived off of this land and these birds were a source of food. In recent years, the wild turkeys nearly became extinct because of hunters and loss of habitat. Fortunately, their population was rescued by conservation efforts that restored the birds' ecological home and by laws that protected them from guns. The turkey's struggle to survive echoes the world's. As the writer Henry Beston said, we and the birds are caught together "…. in the net of life and time, fellow prisoners of the splendor and travail of the earth." Whatever the cause, the rapid changes in life on earth frighten me. At Walden Pond, twenty percent of all the species Thoreau recorded are now locally extinct. I don't like to think of what the air and all that lives in it and breathes its molecules will be like at Little Creek in one hundred years.

My obsession with things avian prompted me to read poetry about birds. I particularly liked poet laureate Ted Kooser's turkey vulture "with wing tips fanned like fingers" and his screech owl, "a bird no bigger than a heart." My favorite nature poet, Mary Oliver, expressed how I felt about finches: "Have you heard them singing in wind above the final fields? Have you ever been so happy in your life?"

In "The Trouble with Poetry," my buddy Billy Collins wrote that "The trouble with poetry is that it encourages the writing of more poetry." That being true, I began to write haiku about the birds I watched: finches in the willows, hummingbirds drinking the sun, herons watching water. In these brief three-line poems, I tried to link nature with human nature.

Picasso said that "[t]he artist is a receptacle for emotions that come from all over the place: from the sky, from the earth, from a scrap of paper, from a passing shape." Toni was a receptacle of emotions that came from the birds in the air, their passing shapes, and the scraps of paper my poems were written on. In a volume bound in soft, dark leather, the accomplished watercolorist painted images depicting the haikus I had written. Under her paintings, she calligraphed my related poems. Writing and painting collaboratively, I believe, allowed us to see things together in a fresh and vivid way, as two children might see them.

At the end of a long August day, finally, the air cooled and turned blue. I was on the lower pond in my canoe looking for a wood duck I'd seen that morning among the cattails and bleached reeds. The water was black and still, very peaceful. To my disappointment, the wood duck was gone. As I paddled along the shore, I heard a familiar noise. I turned my head toward the "rat-ta-ta-tat." In a dead hickory tree, a pileated woodpecker drilled the trunk with its beak. I rested my paddle and let the boat drift. A breeze nudged me closer to the bank. For a while, I watched his scarlet-capped head bob furiously. A community of crows in the woods to the east put up a squawk. Overhead a dark bird, large and lazy, wheeled and drifted on thermal currents. I thought it must be a vulture scavenging. But when I looked closer, I could tell by the tip of its wings it was that red-tailed hawk I often saw. My aversion changed to admiration. There is nothing more picturesque than the flight of a hawk rising and falling with the contour of the wind, guiding himself by the turn of a tail feather. I inhaled deeply. The air that filled my lungs was sweet and rich with the scent of summer.

You will find something more in woods than in books.
Trees and stones will teach you that which you can
never learn from masters.

SAINT BERNARD (1090 - 1153)
Epistle

WOOD

Little Creek's thirty acres is a forest of native hardwood trees except for the clearings of the two ponds and the cabin's yard. Everywhere you look there are living pillars of wood that connect the earth to the sky, the known with the unknown, the ephemeral with the infinite. The log cabin perches on a slope engulfed in the foliage of large white oaks and red maples where Toni and I live among the leaves like two swallows in a nest. It is a quiet, solitary place, perfect if you want to find out what you think of yourself.

These trees of Little Creek bring so much to my life it is hard to list all that their wood and leaves provide. The thick one-hundred-and-fifty-year-old poplar walls of the cabin shelter Toni and me from the elements. Hickory cabinets keep our food and dishes clean and safe. The cherry floors are like a fine piece of furniture underfoot. The maples around the house shade us, keep us cool in the summer, and delight our eyes when their leaves turn red in the fall. The firewood I cut from fallen timber warms us when the days turn cool. The single white oak near the porch of the cabin absorbs many pounds of carbon dioxide every year and releases enough oxygen back into the atmosphere to support our breathing needs. In our state of isolation, the trees along with the birds that nest in them are our friends and closest neighbors. I visit them daily: the big grandfatherly beech deep in the woods, the hawthorn sisters near the lower pond, the dogwood with three trunks joined like Siamese triplets, the "elbow" oak near the creek, the sumacs and crabapples by the road.

One Sunday morning in June when the woods were cool, I hiked to a giant beech that uprooted the previous winter on the shore of the upper pond. As if it were my pew in a forest church, I sat on a bench I had made from a slab of rough-sawn oak. A choir of birds in full voice serenaded me with avian psalms. In the dark water, a reflection of trees sparkled in the sunlight like a stained-glass window.

Usually, when I came here to be alone, I brought *Walden* or something meditative like *Peace is Every Step* in order to read a few pages and get myself pointed in a direction of mindfulness and simplicity. But on that particular day, all I had was a mug of strong coffee and concerns about family matters. I hadn't heard from my daughters in a while, and I was worried about them. I lay back on the bench and looked up through the branches that formed a canopy above me. I rested my arms loosely at my side and let my legs hang freely. I closed my eyes and relaxed my muscles so that I felt as if I were sinking into a silk pillow. I began to breathe, focusing all of my attention on my inhalations and exhalations. After a while, I opened my eyes and looked through a filigree of leaves at patches of pale blue sky that melded perfectly with the viridian foliage. The sunlight transilluminated leaves to varying degrees, creating hues of mint and moss, every shade of green imaginable. I saw things more clearly than I had before. When I returned to the house, I called my daughters and learned that they were all right.

Because the trees were so vital to our lives, I wanted to interact with their wood in an intimate way, to get to know the bark and grain, to make something wooden that would honor the tree it came from.

When I was a Boy Scout, I had done a little woodworking, turning rudimentary bowls and lamps on a lathe in the basement to qualify for a merit badge. However, like the clarinet, chemistry set, archery bow, chessboard, and other things I had tried as a kid and abandoned, I hadn't pursued woodcraft. So I knew my venture with wood should be something simple. I decided to make an end table out of a log, a project that required no expertise with tools but when finished would provide a solid place to set my glass while I watched birds flit among the trees at sunset.

Bill Poole n' Sons sawmill was five minutes away in the little settlement of Helmsburg, located between Doris's general store, which sold bait and beer, and the For Bare Feet sock factory. I drove there on a sunny September afternoon in my old forest-green Lexus SUV, once a classy passenger vehicle that had been right at home in the parking lot of the country club where I played golf. But, like me, it had made the transition from club to country. It served as mud-splattered pickup truck with a hundred thousand miles on the odometer and the smell of dog on the leather seats.

Poole's main building was a massive metal shed that housed saws with blades five feet in diameter, a forklift, and pallets of fresh-cut planks of native hardwoods. The dusty air smelled grainy. It was a pleasant place to be if you liked wood.

In a cluttered corner office eating sandwiches at a rolltop desk, I found Bill and his grown son, Willie, who, many years ago, had set the logs of our cabin and carved his initials in them. Bill was a big man with sloping shoulders and a sagging face topped with a flattop of white hair. He wore bib overalls over a T-shirt that revealed beefy, woodcutter's arms. When I leaned through the doorway, he eyed me somewhat suspiciously and told me I'd have to wait until they were finished with lunch before we could talk about whatever it was I wanted. While he took his time with his meal, I read a newspaper article from the *Brown County Democrat* that was taped to the wall. The piece told about Bill and the history of the sawmill. It began by saying that "Brown County has always lived by its trees, whether painted in their glory or harvested as timber." It went on to say that Bill had always been around trees, working in an apple orchard as a boy, owning a Christmas tree farm, and finally buying the mill in the sixties. His specialty was custom work, such as cutting timber for log cabins like the one he and his wife lived in and like ours at Little Creek. It quoted Bill as warning loggers not to clear cut the land because the woods is more pleasing to look at when only thinned out, and that down the road, in the not-too-distant future, you can have another harvest. I thought if everyone followed his advice and wasn't so damned greedy and impatient, the world wouldn't be in the fix it was in with the planet burning itself up.

Bill wadded up the wax paper his sandwich had been wrapped in and tossed it in the wastebasket—a set shot like the basketball player the newspaper said he once was. "Now, what can I do you for?" he said.

To try to be friendly, I started off by telling them where I lived and asking Willie if he was the one who did the log work on my cabin.

"I reckon so," he said without elaborating.

I gave up on small talk and told Bill I wanted a piece of walnut so I could make a table. He shambled from the office without comment or facial expression that would reveal his opinion of me or my project. He grabbed a big Stihl chain saw with a long blade and checked it for oil and gas. Then he pulled the cord to make sure it would start. When it coughed to life, he shut it off and led me into the lumberyard's world of wood. Oaks, walnuts, cherries, maples, beeches, hickories, and poplars—majestic logs, long and straight with the bark still on them, were stacked two stories high in groups according to species.

I selected a log of black walnut with a diameter of about fourteen inches and a knot that I thought would make an interesting feature. Bill told me to back my car close to the log so it wouldn't have to be carried very far. I did what he asked, but when I left the motor running, Bill said, "Turn that damned thing off. I don't want to smell them fumes."

Embarrassed, I shut the engine down, thinking that in spite of good intentions, I was leaving my own significant carbon footprint on the earth.

I wanted the table to be twenty inches high. I asked Bill to make the cut accordingly. Without measuring, he bent over and let a gob of spit drop from his mouth onto the log to mark where he thought the cut should be. It didn't look right, so I pointed at a spot a few inches away.

"Make it here," I said.

"Ain't twenty," he said. "That's eighteen inches. Move your finger."

I felt like a tenderfoot who couldn't do anything right in Bill's eyes.

The saw let out a howl as its chain ate though the hard, dark walnut, sending up wood-flakes that snowed on the bib of Bill's overalls. I watched the expression on his face as he hunched forward, concentrating on the whirling chain and the incision it was cutting in the log. He wasn't smiling, but I could tell he was alive in the moment and satisfied to be doing what he was doing, just as I once was in an operating room. The hunk of wood thudded to the ground and rolled to my feet. The sun was bright overhead and illuminated the rich colors of the rough-cut cross section. The rings of the heartwood were dark, nearly black, the sapwood russet. Beneath the bark, the narrow cambium layer that once carried nutrients and water to the limbs and leaves was pale yellow. It was a beautiful thing.

"Can I lift it?" I asked.

"I don't know," Bill said. "Are you strong?"

"Not very," I said. "I'm sixty-eight years old."

"So am I," Bill said.

He looked at me with a grin. For the first time, I felt we had something in common, and that for some reason he had decided to accept me. I bent over and wrapped my arms around the big chunk of wood, afraid that I was going to embarrass myself by not being able to lift it.

"We might be the same age," I said. "But you're a hell of lot stronger than I am."

"Then move out of the way," he said.

I did, gratefully, and with a grunt and a red face, the big lug hoisted the log that must have weighed in the neighborhood of a hundred pounds into the back of my vehicle. I worried about how I was going to handle it when I got home, with no one but Toni and Oscar to help me.

"Thanks," I said. "What do I owe you?"

"I don't know. Fifty dollars, I reckon."

When I paid him, I told him that I had a beech tree down on my property that I wanted to make another tabletop out of, but my saw wasn't long enough to cut it. If I drove him and his big saw there, would he do the job? My place was just up the road. "Naw," he said, but with a smile. "I'm getting too old to mess with stuff like that."

At first I was deflated by his rejection, but as I thought about it on the way back to my cabin, I knew what he meant, because I felt that way, too. There were a lot of things I didn't want to mess with anymore. So I didn't take his response personally.

Thich Nhat Hanh once advised an artist to approach a flower he was going to paint with no intention of exploiting it or profiting from it. He likened it to being with a friend without trying to get something from the friendship. That is how I decided to approach the log.

To educate myself about the treatment of wood, I went to the county library and borrowed *The Wood Finisher's Handbook and The Encyclopedia of Woodworking Techniques*. But reading about it didn't tell me all I wanted to know, so I called Rick Ryan, who knew just about everything there was to know about wood. I told Rick I wanted the wood to speak for itself and to not look plastic or artificially glossy. He recommended Danish oil, a polymerized linseed oil, known for its natural, satin finish. When I asked if I needed to let the wood cure, he advised getting the oil on immediately to help keep the wood from splitting. It was what I wanted to hear. I was anxious to start.

The first step was to remove the bark. I did this by driving a chisel with blows from a claw hammer into the line just inside the cambium layer where it joined the sapwood. Once a separation occurred, I inserted a mason's rock splitter into the crease and wedged off the bark in long strips. To expose the underlying wood was like unwrapping a Christmas present and finding the gift you wished for.

Next came the sanding of the log. I started with a coarse 80-grit paper to knock off the roughest edges and gradually worked down to a fine, 280-grit finishing paper. At first, I used a power tool, but I found I preferred sanding by hand. I had been a tactile surgeon, able to diagnose by passing my hand over the dome of a liver or the capsule of a spleen deep in the belly. Maybe that's why I enjoyed the tactile aspect of sanding. I wore thin rubber gloves in the operating room. Now I worked without gloves. In my new life, the skin of my hands was coarse and tough as leather. So many things about me had changed.

I stopped frequently to wipe the dust away and caress the surfaces of the wood to detect rough spots where more work needed to be done. I decided to leave the scratches from Bill Poole's chain saw in the wood as distress marks. Wood finishing is like writing a good piece of fiction. A few flaws in the characters make them more believable and interesting. These imperfections somehow made the wood seem more truthful.

Now it was time to apply the Danish oil. I flooded a rag of soft cotton with the viscous liquid and rubbed it into the wood. I didn't think; I just let my hand move slowly in a continuous circular motion timed to the rhythm of my breathing. The crosscut ends of the log were porous and thirsty, sopping up the oil. Soon the scent of oil and wood rose in the air and mingled to create a rich fragrance, sweet and resiny. The work was as simple as child's play, but it satisfied me. I took my time because I wanted it to last and to be done well.

After the first coat had dried for half an hour, I applied a second coat of oil that I allowed to set for ten minutes. Then I wiped it off with a clean piece of cloth and left the log in the sun to dry. But I couldn't leave the wood alone. I kept coming back to admire it. I liked the smooth, oily surface, the gleam of it. Toni came down from her studio, where she was painting a landscape, to see what I had done. She marveled at the beauty of the finish and complimented me for what I had accomplished. She had a habit of making me feel good about myself. Her approval brought a smile to my face. But I knew I really hadn't done much, stripped a little bark, splashed a little oil around. It certainly wasn't art. I was only acting as a conduit between nature and man. But on second thought, isn't that what an artist is? A conduit. At least that's something someone once said about Paul Cezanne.

Before long, the heat of the sun had an aromatic effect on the wood, creating a perfume that attracted yellow jackets and bumblebees. They swarmed about the wood and kept me away because of my allergy to their venom. I thought of spraying repellent around the log to ward them off. But wood, like the earth, doesn't belong to me or to anyone. I decided it was a bee's right to enjoy the log as much as mine.

Later in the day the sun set and the air cooled and stilled. I went to where the log was resting near our garden behind the cabin. The evening was quiet except for the fuss of two finches fighting for the last sunflower seeds of the day. In the trees, not a leaf or twig moved. For quite a while, I stood, looking deeply at the table. It was no longer merely a log. The wood had been transformed into something beautifully variegated with the rich velvety shades of the forest. When I looked at the wood, I saw the sun and the rain and the cloud the rain fell from, because no tree can grow without water and light. I saw the walnut the tree sprouted from a half century ago. I saw the parent tree the nut fell from. The log's knot looked like the face of an old man with a wrinkled forehead and dark eyes. It seemed I was looking at the face of the logger who timbered the tree and the face of Bill Poole who sawed the log. I saw myself there, too, in the shining wood.

The best man is like water.
Water is good: it benefits all things and does not compete with them.
It dwells in lowly places that all disdain.
This is why it so near to Tao.

LAO-TZU (604 BC - 531 BC)

WATER

We come from water and we are water. Our ancestors, thousands of years ago, were marine creatures submerged in a primordial ocean. Even in our evolved state, our blood remains a saline solution that moves like the tides. My cells swim in a solution of salty lymph like plankton in the sea.

At Little Creek, two man-made ponds have been gouged out of a deep ravine that runs down the middle of the property. Just as the sun is the earth's heart, these small lakes are the land's heart, their water the blood that flows through the veins and arteries of all that lives there. The two ponds are roughly the same size, fifty yards wide and one hundred and fifty yards long, with a combined surface area of about three acres. Their depths, dictated by the height of the dams and the vertical drop of the hollows, are forty feet at the deepest. This depth keeps the water cool during hot summer days, gives it clarity, and lessens the likelihood of algae and other unwanted plant growth. The banks are steep hills that slope up from the shoreline several hundred feet. The runoff of rain from these hills is the source of water that keeps the ponds full and fresh.

Because effects from glaciers and other geological causes humped up the land into rugged hills, Brown County's underground streams are far beneath the earth's crust, and drilling a well is expensive and difficult. Therefore, the ponds were chosen to be the source of Little Creek's drinking water. A submerged electric pump is tethered to the dock of the upper pond. This mechanical device sucks water into a plastic pipe that runs underground up a hill and enters the utility shed of the cabin. There the water flows into a purification system through a microfilter to remove sediment. A solution of chlorine is pumped into it to kill bacteria. The water then passes through a charcoal filter to dechlorinate it and make it taste better. Finally, it is held in a pressure tank, where it waits to wash our dishes, bathe our bodies, become our ice cubes, and nourish the flowers and vegetables in our gardens.

After the water has completed its tasks, it evaporates into the atmosphere, where it condenses into a cloud and waits to return to earth. When the rain falls, the water becomes part of everything again, including the sheet of paper these words are written on and the hand that holds it. Scientists call this sequence the hydrologic cycle. I prefer to think of it as an endless loop of inter-being.

An old Chinese proverb says, "When you drink the water, remember the spring." When I drink the water at Little Creek, I remember the ponds.

Often before dinner on warm summer evenings, I take a fly rod to the dock of the upper pond. I climb into the eight-foot Walker Bay dingy that Toni gave to me for Christmas. It is a charming little boat, my own movable island that I can take to wherever I want to be on the water.

I am not a great fly caster. I know little of hatches and nymphs. But as a surgeon, I do know knots, not angler's knots like a Bimini twist or an Albright special, but the knots of my profession. I like tying flies to the line's monofilament tippet with the one-handed knot I once used when sewing up a laceration or an abdominal incision. In a small way, to have my fingers working takes me back to the operating room.

It is easier to catch a bluegill or a largemouth bass with a night crawler and spinning rod than with a fly. However, there is something less respectful and spiritual about bait casting. My reason for being on the pond was not to haul in a mess to fry or a trophy fish. Rather, I fished because it relaxed me and the line from my rod connected me with the water and the world in its depths.

At dusk on Memorial Day, with pink peonies in bloom, I went to the garage for my fly rod and fishing vest. I took a moment to look at a collage of photographs of my mom and dad that hung on the wall above my workbench. I remembered fondly our togetherness and how Daddy had taught me to fish when I was boy. I tied a Michigan bug to the leader of my fly rod and set sail in the dingy. Before I began to cast the fly, I rowed the little white boat around the pond to get the lay of the water and see where the fish might be feeding. The surface of the pond was an interface between the earth and the sky. The water received its greens and browns from the leaves and bark of hardwoods on the shore. The sky provided blues and the sun's yellowness. The evening was warm. A profound calmness settled onto the water. Crickets sang from the land. Marsh treaders and broad-shouldered water striders skittered on the surface. A turtle as big as a hubcap slid off a log. Frogs leaped into the water. A wood duck fled its nest. Dragonflies clung to cattails that fringed the shore. I felt a sense of peace in every dip of the oar.

The Euro-American metaphor for time is a river with events happening and passing on downstream. But Native Americans believed time was like a pond and events were ripples on the surface. There on the water, lost in my thoughts, time took on a different dimension. My life seemed like a circular wavelet spreading in every direction until it disappeared.

Near a submerged log, I spotted dimples on the surface created by fish nipping at mayflies. I rested my oars and picked up the fly rod. A sense of anticipation arose in me. From the reel, I stripped out enough line to reach the log. Supposedly, a great fly fisherman can think like a fish, and before he casts, he puts himself in the mind of a trout or a tarpon. But the minds of these aquatic creatures were as much a mystery to me as the minds of people I thought I had known but didn't. I whipped the rod back and forth between ten o'clock and two, the line looping and whistling, the fly skimming above the water. On the third cast, a fish hit the fly the moment it touched the surface. Enjoying the bend of the rod, I kept its tip high and the line taut. I retrieved the fish slowly and let it play a little game of tug-of-war with me before I hoisted him or her into the boat. The bluegill floundered on the floor gasping for breath. Careful to avoid the spikes of the dorsal fin, I picked the fish up. With a hemostat borrowed from my surgical practice, I extracted the hook. As if dissecting a thyroid gland, I did it carefully so as not to damage the lip. In a world enamored with "big"—big houses, big cars, big people, big money, big everything—it wasn't much of a fish. The bluegill was a little smaller than my hand, but a fine creature nonetheless, with a golden belly and a black beauty mark behind the gills. Its slivery scales glimmered like a suit of lights. The fish fixed an eye on me and its mouth frowned. I returned my catch to its watery home and watched it swim happily away.

It was early June. The spring at Little Creek had been exceptionally wet. The gray clay was saturated, the ponds filled to the brim, their overflow pipes spewing out a continuous murky stream. Every night, it seemed, we were lulled to sleep by the ping of rain on the roof and a wet wind rustling the trees. Although the precipitation was good for the garden, it wasn't good for me. I had been planning to build stone steps from the porch to the dock below. The daily deluge was keeping me indoors and away from what I wanted to do. Boredom set in, along with a good case of cabin fever. I could only read and write so much. I yearned to be outside, physically active and constructive. Every day I looked at the sky, hoping the rains would stop, but sheets of water kept coming down.

On Saturday evening, June eighth, the rain became a different rain, meaner and more menacing. After Toni and I went to bed, thunder began to rattle the windows, and jagged streaks of lightning snarled and flashed in the sky like the teeth of an angry dog. The air smelled damp and electric. Branches of trees that surround the cabin cracked in wind. Would a limb crash down on the cabin? Suddenly, the drum of the rain against the roof decreased. I relaxed, thinking the storm was letting up. But in a minute or two, the falling water pounded the shingles even louder than before. It was as if I were back in a bunker in Vietnam during the monsoon season. Normally unfazed by storms, Oscar whined and fretted in his crate beside the bed.

I am often asked, "Aren't you afraid, living in such isolation?" Mark Twain said, "None but a coward dares to boast that he has never known fear." I admit I have my fears: losing my mind as my father has, estrangement from my daughters, being alone without Toni, time passing too quickly, ending up a burden. At times I fear death because I don't know what death is. The idea of becoming nothing haunts me. That there is no pain in nothingness is little consolation. In regard to Little Creek, I was sometimes, but not often, mildly afraid when it was dark and I heard noises coming through the woods that I couldn't identify. But I tried to not let my fears imprison me. However, that night, as I lay awake listening to the storm rage, real fear began to stir in me. Will the road be flooded? Will we lose our power? Will the dam give way? Will lightning strike us? I didn't pray for the storm to cease, however, because I don't believe in prayer for personal favors. Also, I didn't believe God was up there with his hand on a spigot. I merely closed my eyes and tried to sleep. But who can sleep when he knows the water is rising outside his door?

I was still awake when the sky began to turn pale gray in the first light of morning. I rose from the bed. I staggered downstairs, leery of what I might find. I stepped out onto the porch and looked down at the lake. It was not Little Creek's pond, placid and green with the reflection of trees as in a pastoral painting. The upper pond was bloated and dirty. Mud washed off the surrounding hills had turned the water brown and thick. It looked as if you could walk on it from one shore to the other. The top of a big black oak had blown into the pond. The tree's limbs stuck out of the water like tentacles of some aquatic beast. The aluminum canoe was full and ready to sink. The water had risen above the overflow pipe; a small trickle ran over one end of the dam. But hallelujah, the dam had held. When the Biblical flood was over, Noah built an altar, got drunk, and ran around naked. But it was too early for cocktails and too late for nakedness. A victory celebration would have been premature because the rain was still coming down in torrents.

Somewhat relieved, I went back inside to feed the dog and fix coffee.

As I filled a mug with Folgers's special brew, I heard Toni call from upstairs, "Look at the dam."

I flung the screen door open and let it bang behind me. I hustled to the porch rail, amazed at what I saw. In a matter of minutes, the pond had turned from bloated to angry and out of control. A torrent of water poured over the middle of the dam and gushed down its slope, flooding what I call the Indian Camp. A wooden bench and fire pit disappeared in front of my eyes. I pulled on a yellow slicker and walked down the hill through the constant downpour. The grass was wet and slick. I took careful steps so as not slip. The central portion of the dam had become a spillway, a river several feet deep, frothing and roaring, crashing down to the lower pond. Raindrops stung my face. I squinted, watching flotsam and a tree limb sweep over the dam. I wondered what was happening to the pond's residents. Were the fish being washed away? How did they breathe through the mud in the water? What about the frogs and turtles? The tadpoles and snakes? I reminded myself to not let Oscar out for fear he might be swept away, too.

My friend, the author Sena Naslund, once wrote a story titled the "Disobedience of Water." I thought of it as I watched the water wild and out of bounds. It was like mob violence. It was as if the laws of Archimedes and Boyle had lost their jurisdiction. The uncontrolled power of the water was daunting. I didn't see how the earthen embankment could survive. The rain came down harder.

Toni, in rain gear and carrying an umbrella, joined me. We hiked down our lane a third of a mile toward the pond that belonged to our nearest neighbors, Jay and Sue DePew. The road that crossed their dam was the only access to our property. We knew that if it had flooded we were stranded. But Jay had told us that his dam had never been breached. We rounded a curve in the lane and looked down at Jay's pond, a frightening sight. The dam and road were gone, replaced by a turbulent waterfall. His dock and rowboat had washed away. I wrapped my arm around Toni's shoulders and we stood there under the umbrella, staring at the torrent flooding the valley below. I thought of Raymond Carver's story "So Much Water So Close to Home." The water roiled. It frothed. It flooded my brain. It was mesmerizing, like watching fire. We both shook our heads.

"What now?" Toni said.

"Time to build an ark," I answered.

Neither of us laughed. We slogged our way back to the cabin to inventory our supplies to see how long we could survive without a trip to the store. In the kitchen, I checked the refrigerator. We had plenty of food but only one gallon of drinking water. I turned on a faucet and filled a glass. I held it up to the window light. I couldn't see through it because it was mud. As Coleridge said, "Water, water, everywhere nor any drop to drink."

Later in the day, the rain slackened. By the next morning, the floodwaters began to recede. The dams on Little Creek were no longer submerged. But the county road at the end of our lane remained flooded. Nearby bridges were underwater, and all the highways in the area were closed and would be for the next three days.

Although we couldn't leave the property, hardships were minimal. When we washed, our clothes and linens turned brown from the sediment in the water. Neither of us felt clean after our showers. We soon ran out of bottled drinking water, but good neighbor Jay brought us a five-gallon carboy. Paul Colvin, a volunteer fireman who lived down the lane, drove up in his truck to see if we were all right or if we needed anything. It was reassuring to know there were people out there who cared and that we were not alone. Their concern made me feel grateful and caused me to look inward.

Electrical power was out almost everywhere in the area, but miraculously ours wasn't. We were able to follow news and weather reports on satellite television. The flood damage was devastating. Southern Indiana was declared a federal disaster area. Hundreds of families near us lost their homes and everything they held precious. Businesses were ruined and crops lost. Bloated dead farm animals were swept downstream. People were rescued from roofs by men in motorboats. High school gymnasiums became shelters and disaster relief centers. Several people drowned in the floodwater. The world seemed cruel and unfair. Like every catastrophe, it begged Job's question: Why were these folks singled out to suffer? Why were we and others spared? It caused me to ponder occasions in my life when it seemed God had let me down—going to war, polio, the death of a girlfriend, the death of Mother, the birth of a disabled child, a divorce. The only way I can explain my belief is to say that He is not my personal God. His role must be something bigger that I don't understand.

October, the dry season, a time of seedpods, berries, falling nuts, and ladybugs. It hadn't rained since late June. As if in compensation for the flood damage, the warm, wet spring and a dry, sunny fall had rewarded Brown County with an autumn of brilliant color. During cool nights, the veins of leaves constricted, and the flow of sugar water that nourished them became obstructed. Chlorophyll green gave way to anthocyanin and carotenoid pigments of saffron, bronze, and scarlet. The beautiful leaves spun down onto the pond and sank, where they decomposed. Their tannins stained the water the color of dark rum and left an oily sheen on the surface.

In the village of Nashville, "leaf peepers" were everywhere, clogging streets with their Harley-Davidsons and "Land Yachts." Oblivious to the cataclysm of a few months ago, they gorged on peanut butter fudge and corn dogs. But in nearby Columbus, the hospital where I practiced surgery had sustained damage from the flood that would cost two hundred million dollars to repair. It remained closed. On the bottomland near the foot of our lane, a humble ranch-style house that had been under water in the spring stood dark-windowed and deserted. A tricycle, toys, mattresses, and the pillows of an old couch were strewn about on a mud-flat yard. A camper shell looked like the corpse of a giant sea turtle.

My dad used to say, "Poor folks have poor luck." Looking at my neighbor's plight, it seemed as though that was true. I don't mean it in a patronizing way. Neither would my father, for he too had known what it was to be poor. Also, I don't believe you necessarily make your luck. You might be able to influence it some, but I believe luck, good or bad, happens randomly. That's why they call it luck rather than accomplishment or failure.

By the front door of the neighbor's flooded home, new two-by-fours were stacked, suggesting that whoever lived there was going to try again, bravely. I'm continually amazed at the resilience of people. Why hadn't I done something to help them?

For the most part, all evidence of the flood had been eradicated at Little Creek. We were back to entertaining guests by feeding the catfish from the dock, and the bluegill were biting. My yardmen had dragged the treetop from the pond and cut it up into firewood. The timbers that lined the gravel beach where Toni's grandkids liked to swim had been replaced. With river stone from Bean Blossom Creek, I filled the washout in the dam. A paver dumped three truckloads of crushed gravel to fill the ruts carved by the floodwater. The pump and filters in the water system that were clogged with mud had been replaced. Our water had regained its clarity. Indian Camp at the foot of the dam was ready again for campfires and marshmallow roasts. I built a tall cairn that looked like a stone person. I called it "Rain Man" to commemorate the flood of 2008.

WATER

Flash forward four years. Of all my summers in Indiana, this is the hottest and driest I can remember. It reminds me of the days during the war when I sweltered in Vietnam's trembling and relentless heat. Day after day, broiling temperatures bake the land. It hasn't rained in a month. Brown County's creek beds have evaporated into pale, sepia-toned streams of rocks, gravel, and sand. To paraphrase Woody Guthrie's Dust Bowl lament, the creeks are "rippling rivers of dust." Hay fields are parched and stubbled. Charcoal rot withers soybean leaves, turning them yellow. Stunted ears cling to the dry skeletons of feed-corn stocks. Crops are plowed under. Cattle go hungry. The roadside stands that sell melons and sweet corn are unmanned and empty-shelved. Farmers sweat and grieve. The Fourth of July fireworks in Nashville are cancelled because of the risk of fire. Barren land. Cracked earth. You can feel the hot dryness in your throat.

At Little Creek, the earth is baked hard as if it were kiln-dried. Thirsty grass in the yard in front of the cabin succumbs and dies of heat exhaustion. Hostas in the gardens shrivel. The sycamores on the shore of the pond shed their leaves as if it were autumn. Grass seeds sowed last spring lie dry and dormant as if they were grains of sand.

To keep the vegetable and perennial gardens alive, we water the plants daily. The sprinkler oscillates to and fro, throwing its rainbowed spray in a losing cause. The weeping cherry, the Mugo pine, and a Japanese maple in my Zen garden die. The stone catch basin is bone dry. The needles of my bonsai tree are pale and parched. The obedient little juniper's demise disheartens me. Even the Buddha would lose his smile.

The heat has made the birds irritable. Tufted titmice and chickadees squabble and peck at each other. Finches fight at the feeder. As they do in winter, the mice have come indoors, but now it is to escape the heat and to find water. The little rodents eat a can of peanuts, paper napkins, two of Toni's T-shirts and a blouse. As a way of payment, they leave their droppings on the pantry shelves. Oscar, with his thick Wheaton coat, is a cool weather creature. In the heat, he becomes lethargic. He no longer gallops down the hill to bark at deer and wild turkeys in the woods. He prefers to lie with his chin on the cabin's cool cherry floors. Toni experiences frequent migraine attacks. Research suggests these headaches might be a result of a heat-induced increase in the production of the hormone serotonin. My hormones are heat sensitive, too. My adrenalin level drops. My endorphins hibernate. I become easily fatigued, apathetic, and a little depressed. I can't write. I forsake my morning jog and spend the afternoons nap-reading in the cabin's air conditioning. A round of golf in the one-hundred-degree heat is out of the question. I keep looking at the western sky, hoping to see cumulonimbus clouds full of rain on the horizon. But all I see are cirrus clouds, high and wispy and rainless. As the blues song goes, "Let it rain. Let it rain. Let it rain. We'll be happy again."

As the drought continues, the water level of the pond drops two feet, and the shoreline becomes dried muck. Last summer I built an eight-plank Yatsuhashi bridge like one in the gardens of Kyoto, Japan. The staggered wooden structure spans the shallows at the far end of the pond. When I dug the postholes and drove the pilings that support the planks, I stood in water up to my knees. Now the bridge crosses a mudflat you could walk across and not wet your shoes.

With the rise in temperature, the ecosystem of the ponds becomes confused and out of sync. Duckweed spouts among cattails. Water lilies desiccate. Filamentous algae flourishes and turns the water a pea-soup green. Bluegill retreat to cooler depths and lose their appetite. But I don't care. It's too damn hot to fish. I begin to wonder if the pond will ever be full again. Existence at rain-starved Little Creek feels threatened.

At the end of the day, Toni and I no longer enjoy a glass of white wine on the porch with the birds. The heat drives us inside to a flat-screen television set. The evening news is grim. The drought and heat waves are worldwide. Greenland's ice sheet melts at a rate not seen in thirty years. Coral reefs are being destroyed. Glaciers recede. Sea levels rise. Rivers run dry.

On the *News Hour,* James Hanson, the NASA climatologist and professor of earth and environmental science at Columbia University, is interviewed. He shows a temperature chart with a bell-shaped curve shoved to the right that demonstrates an undeniable trend of global warming. It is as if we are slowly suffocating ourselves in a gas chamber of carbon dioxide.

"We have a planetary emergency," Hanson says grimly. "If humans continue to burn fossil fuels at the current rate, 20 to 40 percent of species on the planet will become extinct by the end of the century. It's a moral issue."

I try to imagine what Little Creek will be like then. Who will adapt? What will be lost? The turtles? The tulip trees? The salamanders? The songbirds? The willows? The wasps?

Even though we know in our hearts what our addiction to fossil fuel is doing to the planet, we pretend we don't and opt for instant gratification. Oil still trumps water. New drill bits and oil pipes burrow the parched earth like serpents of steel. Oil gushes from a flaming rig into the Gulf of Mexico. The water used in hydraulic fractionation contaminates the water table. Thoreau wrote that "nature is as well adapted to our weakness as to our strength." I believe we are pushing those adaptive powers beyond their limit. I feel the heat of the day and am guilty for my carbon indulgences.

September second. The last day of my seventy-second year on earth. I awaken to the distant kettledrum rumble of thunder. Oscar hears it, too. He barks and frets in his crate beside our bed as he did before the flood. I let him out. With a cup of coffee, I go to the porch and watch dark clouds move up the valley from the west toward the cabin. The sky is low and solid, a tarnished silver dome. The temperature drops. Gusts of cool wind ripple the pond's water and jangle the wind chime that hangs from the cabin's eave. The leaves of the beech trees on the shore of the pond tremble and show their silver bellies. A soft rain begins to fall. Big drops dimple the surface of the pond.

I put on a yellow slicker. With a paper sack of grass seed, I make my way down the parched hill in front of the cabin. I cast the seeds on the lawn's bare spots that I tried to plant last spring. The rain wets my face. A cool, moist balm.

All morning long, the downpour continues. It soaks the earth and pings on the cabin's roof. At noon, Toni and I sit at the picnic table on the porch and eat grilled cheese sandwiches with bacon and sliced tomatoes from the garden. The rain drones on, soft and hypnotic. The drops come down from the clouds on silver threads. Toni remarks that she has always loved to watch rain. I remember when I was boy in my room mesmerized by the rain falling outside the window. Before long the stone catch basin in the Zen garden is filled to the brim. The grass seems greener. The chickadees at the feeder are more animated. The finches chirp happily. The shower cleanses me of melancholy.

To a man who's never laid a stone there's nothing you can tell him. Even the truth would be wrong.

CORMAC MCCARTHY,
from his play, "The Stonemason."

STONE

Evenings at Little Creek in those first days, Toni and I usually shunned the television set. We traded its programs of sensationalism and violence for a swing-seat on the cabin's porch. Each with glass of white wine, we talked about our day, what Toni had painted and what I had written, something we read. We were adapting to the easy pace of our lives. Entertainment was watching goldfinches and tufted titmice flit from the woods in the valley below to the feeders that hung from the eaves. However, the trees blocked our view of a three-acre pond where ducks swam and deer came to drink. With the exception of watching a fire in a fireplace, nothing tranquilizes me quite like gazing at water. To allow a view of the pond's bucolic beauty, I decided to clear some of the trees.

To help me do the timbering, I employed Jason and Jordan, two strapping college football players who mowed my grass. Jason was studying to be a dentist and Jacob a pilot at Indiana State University. We rented a wood chipper. They brought their docile dog, Bear, and a chain saw with a blade long enough to take on big trunks. The three of us spent the next couple of days clearing the hillside of sycamores, silver maples, and small beeches. To waste a living tree caused a guilt pang to pass through me. The feeling

STONE

was akin to what I thought it would be like to shoot a deer, which I have never done and never will. Deer slaying was, to me, almost the same as Thoreau said of hunting snipes and woodcocks: "It would be nobler game to shoot oneself." Well, maybe Henry took it took it too far. I don't own a gun. Like my pacifist father, I am antigun, antiwar, and antiviolence. I saw enough guns and the wounds their bullets caused when I was a battalion surgeon in Vietnam during the war.

The boys and I sawed. We lifted. We lugged the fallen timber. I enjoyed working with young people. I liked to hear about what they were studying, what they were thinking. I tried to encourage them. I admired the boys' strength and stamina. But I didn't covet their youth. To me life is like a baseball game composed of many innings. When an inning is over, don't fret about the score. Just play the next inning.

Jason, Jordan, and I dressed off the limbs from smaller trees and used the trunks to line walking paths we made through the woods and around the pond. We fed the treetops into the chipper and then spread the mulch onto the hiking trails. Returning the wood to the floor of the forest allayed some of my guilt.

After the trees had been cleared, I decided to make a hillside fern and hosta garden to enhance the view from the porch. For that, I needed to build a stone wall with a terrace behind it where the plantings would go. The idea of masonry appealed to me. The laying of stone seemed like elemental work, the same as carving wood, throwing a pot, or weaving with homespun yarn. Stone is a substance as near to eternal as any matter. Maybe laying stone was my attempt at achieving immortality. I say this knowing that it is the fate of every wall to crumble, the destiny of every rock to dissolve back into the sea.

I was aware again of the ice age. During that time not as long ago as we might think, geological forces heaved up the earth of southern Indiana into rugged hills. The Wisconsin glacier came to rest on the northern border of my Little Creek property where Bean Blossom Creek now flows. The rock underlying Little Creek and Brown County is Mississippian-aged sandstone, siltstone, and shale composed of the corpses of sea creatures that lived here more than three hundred million years ago. This bedrock is buried deep beneath the surface of the hills, so there is no fieldstone to collect like the farmers of rural New England gathered to build their walls. I needed quarry stone for the wall I wanted to build.

Southern Indiana is famous for its quarries. A few miles south of Little Creek, between Bloomington and Bedford, is limestone country. The magnificent stone harvested there has been used to build some of the great edifices in the world, including the Empire State Building, the Pentagon, the Metropolitan Museum of Art, the Lincoln Memorial, and many others. But I didn't want limestone. I wanted its country cousin, Brown County stone, a friable brown sandstone. It is a humble rock but beautiful nonetheless and native to where I was living.

Over the telephone, I ordered the stones from a man named Kenny, who owned a quarry in the hills southwest of Nashville, Indiana. I gave him the rough dimensions of the wall. He estimated that six tons of stone would be necessary. *One-hell-of-a-lot of lifting*, I thought, *for an old man. But bring them on.*

"I'm close to seventy years old," I said. "Don't make them all that heavy."

"I'll bring what you can handle," Kenny said.

Early the next morning, Kenny appeared in his dump truck, its bed filled with big chunks of Brown County stone. He backed down the hill to a level spot as close as possible to the site where the wall was to be built. He pushed a button in the cab of the truck. The bed lifted and twelve thousand pounds of rock thundered to the ground. I felt the earth quake. A cloud of stone dust filled the air. I smelled its earthy scent. The power of the rock gave me pause. I knew I was up against something formidable.

Kenny climbed out of the truck and came toward me. He was a short, muscular man, wearing tight jeans and a shirt unbuttoned to reveal a silver cross hanging from a gold chain around his neck. His hair was dyed black and pompadoured. He wore cowboy boots with pointed toes.

"Howdy," he said. "Doc Walker, you operated on my missis."

I couldn't remember her name or the surgery I performed, as was true with many details of my surgical practice. That phase of my life was becoming more and more a part of the past. But I still liked to be remembered as a doctor. I told Kenny I hoped his wife's operation had gone well. He said it had. She was alive and well because of it. Without me asking, he informed me that he was a minister.

"What church?" I asked.

STONE

"Nazarene," he said. "But I don't have my own church. The world's my church. How about you? Where do you go to church?"

Although I had been baptized and sent to Sunday school, I no longer went to church except for weddings and funerals or to admire the architecture and stained glass. For me there was no need for temples or complicated doctrine. As the Dali Lama said, the philosophy to follow is simple: "Be kind."

"Right here's my church," I said, only half in jest. "The great outdoors. This wall I'm going to build is an altar of sorts."

Kenny looked skeptical. Before he left, he told me he was preaching that night at a tent meeting down by the village of Gnaw Bone. He asked me if I would like to come. For a moment, curiosity made me consider his offer, but I begged off. The stone-man evangelist left disappointed.

After he drove away, I turned and looked at the six-ton pile of rock. The stones looked huge and heavy. I wondered if I was strong enough to do the work. I took a deep breath. I pulled on a pair of leather work gloves and began.

After some research, I had decided to build a dry-laid stone wall where the masonry is held together by gravity rather than by mortar. Kenny might say what holds the rocks is the thumb of God pressing down. The first step was to dig a two-foot wide trench, deep enough to partially bury the first course of stone. For several hours, I hacked away at the hill with a landscaper's pick to break up the rock-hard red clay, or terra rossa, as geologists call it. I then shoveled the loose dirt up the hill for backfill. It was hot. I was not in stonemason's shape. But I kept at it without taking a break because I wanted to see some stones in place. It was like hurrying through your dinner to get to dessert. The antithesis of Buddhism.

When the trench was dug, I began to lay the foundation. I used the largest and longest stones in the pile first. I worked from the ends into the middle and stepped the rocks to accommodate the side slope of the hill and create a level layer. I checked my work with an old wooden carpenter's level bought at a flea market. I was pleased when its air bubble floated between the middle marks. Satisfied I'd done my level best, I began the second course of stone. I staggered the joints so that a full stone sat above the juncture of two stones beneath it. "One stone over two, two over one" is the rule of the stonemason. A bondstone is a long rock that spans the wall's width. Every few feet, I placed such a stone to tie the wall together. For stability, it was recommended that the wall slope into the hill at a ratio of two inches for every foot of height. To guide me, I had made a batter gauge out of strips of wood nailed together in the shape of a scalene triangle. Its vertical leg equaled the wall's height, and the horizontal leg equaled the slope. As the rock rampart grew higher, I held the batter to its face to check my angle. When I was satisfied with the slope, I tapped small rocks and chips into gaps with a mason's hammer. I had to be careful not to dislodge the rocks already set. An anvil-like ring rose in the air. A prehistoric sound echoed through the valley as metal struck stone. I felt like a Stone Age man.

Day after day I worked on the wall. Each night I climbed into bed dog tired. I would lie awake thinking of the stones. It was the way I once laid awake rehearsing the anatomy of the operation I was to perform the following morning. Admittedly, the stakes were higher back then, but the stones had taken on a special meaning and importance to me. I arose early and started to work when the sun was still low behind easterly trees. I wanted to lay as much stone as I could before it became hot. Only the birds and squirrels were there to watch me, alone in the woods. The caw of crows egged me on. Sweat-drenched and dirty, I took my time with each rock. There was a human quality, a persona, to every stone. Some were faceted, some round and smooth, some brown, some orange-ish. Each one had a heft of its own. The more experienced I became, the better I could visualize the shape and size of the rock that was needed next. I was like the old limestone cutter who once said, "I want the stones to fit like a key in a lock." To lift a stone satisfied me. I am an aging man who has lost thirty percent of his muscle mass. Winning the struggle with a rock somehow blunted my deterioration. At times, however, I grew tired. My biceps quivered. My back hurt. Moving from wall to rock pile, I felt like Sisyphus must have felt on his way down the mountain.

"You son of a bitch," I would call a particularly heavy rock.

When it was in place, I forgave it.

Finally, the wall had risen to the height I wanted it to be. My emotions were mixed. I wanted to see the wall finished, but I didn't want the work to end. I capped off the top with flat stones that were as broad as possible and fit together well. I hoped that water would drain off them. I didn't want ice forming between the stones and prying them apart. I planned to backfill the wall with topsoil and plant a bed of hostas and ferns. But for now there was just a wall of rock. It stood alone like some Neolithic monument. The rocks conveyed a primal feeling of order and strength. I walked around the wall and ran my hand over the surfaces. The stones felt warm from the heat of the day and granular. Camus wrote that "[a] face that toils so close to stones is already stone itself." Had I become stone? I didn't feel like it. I felt light, almost buoyant. In spite of my fatigue, my heart was full, and I was happy. I called Toni to show her the finished product.

"Oh, sweetheart," she said. "Look what you've done."

Ah.

A few days later Kenny stopped by to drop off his bill and to see what I had accomplished. He said the wall looked damned good. These days he couldn't get anyone to do stone work. He wondered if I would consider building some walls for his customers. The pay would be thirty dollars an hour. I could work whenever I wanted to. I was flattered and my head swelled up, but I told him my stone-laying days were over. I have to say, however, I believe that stonework is a calling. I would be proud to be known as a stonemason.

The path Jason, Jordan, and I had created looped deep into an unspoiled forest of native hardwood. The rugged route often followed deer trails marked by scat and the prints of cloven hooves. Even on the hottest days of summer, it was cool in the woods. I liked to go there in the afternoon when Toni was painting in her studio. I enjoyed working alone on the path. I cut away prickly greenbrier vines and pruned overhanging branches. Sometimes I took a book along and found a place to sit and read. Sometimes I just sat and wondered. One day in a dry streambed, I discovered some fine stones washed smooth by centuries of flowing water. Their surfaces were muted shades of brown that answered to the sun's shifting light. Lichens and green moss grew on their surface and softened them. The stones seemed to be asking to be part of a monument. I thought I should grant them their request and build a cairn. On the bank of the streambed, I spied a level shelf of ground I thought would be a good site. The stack of stones could serve as a milestone marker on the path the way cairns have marked the trails of the Inuit, the Aborigines, the Greeks, the Potawatomi Indians, and almost every civilization known to man.

The gully was steep and narrow. I had to climb over a waist-high log each time I lugged a rock up to the construction site. But I didn't mind. There was no hurry to finish, no other place I had to be. Wilderness surrounded me, and above was a flawless blue sky. I had taken two tumbles recently on slick hills that required treatment to sore body parts with ice packs and Advil. Alone in the woods, there was no one around to help me if I fell and injured myself. So I climbed the steep, rocky creek bed with cautious steps. After I accumulated a large pile of stones of varying shapes and sizes, I paused a moment to catch my breath. I sat on a log and looked around. I saw a snake coil under a rock and disappear. The leaves of a shagbark hickory shone gaunt and gold. Limbs sighed in a breeze. I thought how much would be lost if these trees were destroyed. We needed them if for no other reason than to have a quiet, shady place to walk.

When I was rested, I began the cairn by laying a circle of stones on the ground with a diameter of about three feet. On this foundation, I built concentric layers of flat rocks. Each stratum was smaller than the underlying one. I hadn't worked with stone since I built the wall. It felt good to be a mason again. The work came easily to me. It didn't seem like work. When I was satisfied with the height of the structure, I capped the cairn with a stone the size and shape of my head. I walked slowly around the mound of rock. I admired it from various angles, trying to decide what to name it. In England, piles of rocks used to mark hiking trails are called "duckies." But "duckie" didn't seem right. I'd have to think about it.

At dusk Toni and I took an evening walk on the path. The woods were quiet except for Oscar's bark. He was unhappy to be left alone at the cabin. I led Toni past a giant beech tree and down the steep embankment to the new cairn.

"It is a Buddha," she said.

It has been said that whether you see the Buddha or not depends on you. I looked more deeply at the stones. I, too, saw the Buddha, squat, round-bellied, smiling in the wilderness.

All the sounds of the earth are like music.

OSCAR HAMMERSTEIN II

SOUND

The sounds of Little Creek are miracles of physics, physiology, and neurochemistry. To contemplate them takes me back to medical school and what I learned about hearing. Each Little Creek sound starts with vibrations that become waves. This energy may be created by air rushing through the folds of tissue in a finch's windpipe or Oscar's vocal cords. The wind stirring the leaves of an oak tree or raindrops pelting the log cabin's shingles cause waves of energy to travel through the air in all directions like the ripples from a pebble dropped into the pond. When the sound waves arrive at my ears or Toni's or Oscar's, they are funneled through an auditory canal to miniature drums covered by tympanic membranes. The vibrations that move our eardrums' paper-thin skins are amplified by the three tiniest bones in our bodies: the incus (the hammer), the malleus (the anvil), and the stapes (the stirrup). Pressure fluctuations of these ossicles are then transformed into electrical impulses in our inner ears by our cochleae, snail-like chambers filled with watery fluid and lined by tiny sensory hair cells. From our cochleae, signals are transmitted by the auditory nerve to our brains. There they become the melodies of Little Creek's wildlife, wind, and water. I think of these sounds as the

SOUND

music of the planet Earth.

One cold, golden morning in October, the first frost of the season whitewashed the grass. I was wakened by Oscar barking at two does that often visit the dam. I arose and filled his dish with holistic dog food. (He alternates between a duck blend and one made of salmon, anchovies, and sardines. Toni believes these pricey gourmet concoctions are good for his skin.) The ping of pellets hitting the metal of his bowl sent him into a gleeful frenzy. I made the coffee. As it brewed, I heard a happy growl and gurgle. I hung the bird feeders and started a fire in the woodstove. With a cup of coffee, I sat in front of the flames beside Toni. She read a novel from her Kindle. I read Thoreau's account of sound at Walden Pond. His world whizzed, rattled, rang, echoed, hooted, moaned, lowed, crowed, crackled, snapped, screamed, bellowed, hissed, and cried. I could hear Walden as if I were there. It sounded like Little Creek.

The passage of time at the cabin is marked by sounds—a train's whistle at 4:00 am, the tick and gong of a regulator clock, the awakening two-note trill of a cardinal that fills me with inner delight. In front of the fire, the tick and hiss from burning logs and the creak of the stove's iron box expanding in the heat marked the passing of time. But time seemed irrelevant. We had nothing planned.

After the sun had risen, I pulled on a fleece jacket and made my way through a hushed woods to the bench on the shore of the lower pond. Along the way, leaves crunched underfoot. They whispered the sound of autumn's footsteps. I went to the pond seeking quiet and to escape the dissonance of my mind. In the sunlight, trees reflected on the water and shone with hues from the leaves: the oak's russet, the maple's and sumac's scarlet, the beech's lemon yellow. Brilliant and gaudy, the colors created a cacophony of light. Inspired by Thoreau's treatise on sound that I had just read, I chose an acoustic rather than an optic meditation. I closed my eyes to listen. The sounds I heard amazed me. It was like finding tiny mushrooms, moss, or wildflowers that I had never noticed before. The voices of the woods and water called to me. I heard the dry hiss of leaves in a light breeze, the music of water trickling into the pond's overflow pipe, a frog's splash as it leaped from the shore, the tap of a woodpecker's beak drilling a tree trunk. Suddenly blasts from a hunter's gun came from over a hill to the east.

SOUND

The rude bangs smashed into the anvils of my ears and echoed through the valley. The explosions triggered the neurochemical magic of my memory. For an instant, I was transported back to my time in Vietnam and the war's blood, bullets, and bombs. Now I kept my eyes closed and just shook my head in disgust and disappointment. From a distance came the mournful bay of Sugar, our neighbor's chocolate lab.

Everything was quiet for a moment, and then I heard the forlorn chirp of a single cricket. I knew a cricket's life span was brief, about three weeks for a male and less for females. They die after laying their eggs. I also knew that it is the male who does the chirping. He woos the female by rubbing his forewings together as if they were bow and strings. The chirping I heard slowed and became a kind of death rattle. I thought the poor guy must be near his demise. I couldn't help but contemplate my own mortality and death's accompanying sounds. When would the "lub-dub" of my heart and the lisp of my lungs stop? What sounds would I make before I entered the silence of eternity or nothingness? A bird chirped like a pulley that needed oil. It was answered by an operatic avian trill that raised me happily from my grave.

While waiting for guests to arrive from Indianapolis for a picnic lunch, I was in the driveway, throwing a stick for Oscar to chase. Suddenly, the dog dropped the length of wood from his mouth. He cocked his head and pricked his ears. I listened for the sound that had put him on guard, but I heard nothing. Oscar's sense of hearing is more highly developed than mine. He can register twice as many frequencies as I can. His auditory range is four times longer than my ten-octave spread. Because of his acute canine hearing, Oscar had become the early warning system for Little Creek. Now he alerted me like a typical terrier. He barked frantically in a brassy voice interspersed with guttural growls. After a few seconds, I was aware of the crunch of tires on gravel. Soon a silver van appeared among the trees. I smiled and waved at the familiar, much-loved passengers in the car.

My Uncle Puff hoisted himself out of the driver's seat. At eighty-one, Puff is the youngest and only survivor of my father's six siblings. He opened the car door for his wife, Aunt Doris. Both are young in appearance. They are a tidy and attractive couple with fair Scotch-Irish complexions. Puff looked spiffy in a pressed plaid summer shirt and khakis. Doris wore a lightweight pants suit. Last out of the car was their daughter, my cousin, Lou Ann Walker. Her pale complexion and long auburn hair shone in the sunlight. She is a writer and editor from New York. Some time ago, her husband, Speed Vogel, a favorite of mine, had died after a long and trying illness. I was pleased to see Lou Ann smiling again.

Oscar circled about and wagged his tail while we all exchanged hugs. I told Lou Ann how glad I was to see her. But no words were exchanged between me and my aunt and uncle because they are deaf. Puff greeted me with a hand to the forehead salute, the sign for "hello." His cheerful smile belied the adversities he has faced because of his deafness. He acquired his loss of hearing before he was three months old when an infection destroyed his auditory nerves. Doris lost her hearing to spinal meningitis when she was thirteen months old. They met at the Indiana School for the Deaf and have spent their lives together in love and silence. In spite of their deafness, a disability Helen Keller found to be a greater handicap than her blindness, Puff and Doris have led a full and significant life in a world of sounds that is, at times, hostile toward those who can't speak or hear. Puff earned their living as a linotype operator for the *Indianapolis Star,* a job often done by the deaf because the noise of the machinery doesn't bother them. Doris was at home, raising their three extremely bright daughters. The girls are all grown now and accomplished. They hold degrees from Smith, Butler, and Harvard.

To begin their visit, we climbed the steps to Toni's studio in the barn's loft, where the white beadboard walls are hung with her oil landscapes and watercolor botanicals. Doris, with her enhanced visual powers, had a special appreciation of the shapes and colors of Toni's work. She was effusive in her praise for the paintings. She expressed herself with gestures and smiles and a humming noise that came from low in her larynx.

When it was lunchtime, we gathered on the porch at the picnic table that Toni had covered with a yellow flowered cloth. A bouquet of Queen Anne's lace and black-eyed Susans was the centerpiece. The day was warm, the air filled with the noises of summer that go unnoticed even to the hearing unless they think to listen: the chirr of cicadas, the murmur of bees, the moan of mourning doves. Our paddle fans stirred the air with a sea-breeze whisper. Chickadees burbled and finches fussed noisily at a bird feeder. Toni made a chilled lunch of bean and asparagus salad and cold beef tenderloin.

SOUND

Puff chose a Heineken. Toni and Doris drank Chardonnay. Lou Ann and I settled for iced tea. Oblivious to the clink of cubes and glasses, Puff raised his bottle in appreciation of the taste of cold beer and fellowship with his family.

Since Lou Ann was a child, she had been her parents' voice and ears in the hearing world. She documented the experience poignantly in her acclaimed and moving memoir, *A Loss for Words: The Story of Deafness in a Family*. As we ate, Lou Ann held her fork in one hand and with her other hand continuously carried the conversation to and from her parents by American Sign Language. I loved to watch their fingers move gracefully and quickly, pulling words out of the air like a magician pulling silk scarves from a sleeve. They used facial expression and body movement to help make themselves understood. I regret that I never learned sign language. I feel I have let Puff and Doris down. But they are both gentle souls, tolerant and accepting. I doubt they are critical of me. I know they wouldn't want me to feel guilty.

Because of my inability to sign, Puff and I communicate by scribbling notes to each other on scraps of paper. It is a poor substitute for signing, but it does allow us to communicate in a limited way. After a dessert of fresh raspberries and brownies, I wrote an invitation for him to join me on the shore of the pond to spin cast for bluegill and bass. He seemed reluctant at first, but he knew I wanted him to fish. To please me, he nodded in agreement. On the dock, I baited a hook with a cricket and cast it into the pond, then handed him the rod. Standing in the void of his deafness, he peered intently at the orange bobber floating on the dark water. A proud man, he tried hard to be a perfect angler, just as he had tried hard at everything all of his life. At times when I'm watching my daughter, Sarah, in her wheelchair, I try to imagine what it would be like to not walk or run, to never have done either. As I watched Uncle Puff poised with the rod in his hand, I was aware of the sounds he couldn't hear: crows creating a ruckus—caw, caw, the sound from a hawk wheeling high overhead—twee, twee, twee. I heard the claws of a gray squirrel scrape hickory bark. I wondered what it would be like to have never heard a Hoagy Carmichael tune or Cole Porter song or a riff from Wes Montgomery's guitar or the voices of Bruce Nauman's "sound sculpture" at the MOMA. (All Puff's fellow Hoosiers.) In *A Loss for Words*, Lou Ann writes, "It (deafness) is one of the cruelest and most deceptive of afflictions. It can emasculate men and devastate women." Diane Ackerman, in *A Natural History of the Senses,* likened the deaf to roots buried beneath the soil. But as is true with Sarah, Puff shows no bitterness or resentment. There is nothing buried about him.

Suddenly, Puff's bobber disappeared underwater with a slurp. His reel zinged, his pole bent, and he began retrieving his catch. He held the tip of the rod too low and reeled too fast. I was afraid the fish would get away. I wanted to tell him to slow down and raise the rod, but of course he wouldn't have heard me. Puff horsed the fish out on to the dock. It was a bluegill only about five inches long, flipping about and gasping for breath. Puff seemed as pleased with his small catch as if he had landed a hundred-pound tarpon. I gave him a thumbs-up. Before I returned the fish to its watery home, Puff held the little fish by the leader of his line. I used my iPhone camera to snap a picture of my silent hero.

For Toni's seventy-first birthday, I gave her a wind chime with a cherry wood clapper and eight long aluminum tubes that vibrate in their own individual frequencies. Its melodic tenor tones were said to be inspired by Gregorian chants. I hung the chime over the deck of her studio from the limb of a beech tree. I wanted her to hear it ring in the breeze while at her easel. In their tradition, Buddhist monks use the toll of temple bells to bring them back to the present moment. When the monks hear the bells, they stop talking and thinking and return to themselves, breathing and smiling. Sometimes they recite a verse:

"Listen, listen.

This wonderful sound brings me back to my true self."

When I hear the wind stir Toni's chime, I stop and listen and return to my true self.

You can't do anything ....
With a man who likes to chop wood.

ROBERT FROST
In the Orchard

FIRE

Aristotle argued that everything beneath the moon is composed of four elements—fire, air, earth, and water—and everything beyond the moon was ether and imperishable. Of these four elements, the stoics believed fire came first and that eventually everything will be consumed back into fire. I agree that Aristotle and the stoics are right metaphorically. What follows is about fire.

As autumn approached, the days at Little Creek shortened. Restless lambswool clouds appeared high in the sky. The leaves of the sumacs turned saffron, the maples ruby and gold, all brilliant as they prepared to die and drop. Vees of geese honked their way south. Fewer birds appeared at our feeders because they had begun their migrations to the tropics. As the angle between the earth and the sun widened, the strength of the sun's fire weakened. The air became too cool in the morning to go to the bench and read. In a jacket and jeans, I sat in a porch rocker and listened to acorns thud to the ground. Toni painted a watercolor of two maple leaves, veined and variegated in shades of red and yellow. I wrote one of my American haikus to express what her painting

FIRE

evoked in me:

Unafraid maple leaves
flutter on to the pond
I am part water leaves and decay.

I could feel the change of seasons in my bones, a sense of incredibility. Is it really this late in the year? Am I really this old? But I didn't fear or regret the prelude to winter. Nor did I fear old age as much as I once did. I welcomed a new time of year. I was finding the same thing was true with my life. Each phase brought me something unique and pleasurable. As Solomon said in Ecclesiastes, "To everything there is a season, a time for every purpose under the sun." Although I've heard it a thousand times, that's still a great piece of writing. I particularly enjoyed fall because it was football season and a time to gather wood and light a fire.

Monday, October third, was a day of sunshine and leaping winds. The conditions were perfect for harvesting firewood. I dressed in frayed khaki shorts, an old T-shirt, and a sweat-stained ball cap. I had spent a lifetime trying to look good in the eyes of others. I feared rejection and was too concerned with the approval of those who saw me. I dressed well, joined committees, and met with people. I sought out offices to hold, events to attend, and parties to give. I was afraid to be left out and alone. But in recent years, I was coming to the realization that if I couldn't be happy with and by myself, then happiness wasn't within my reach. At Little Creek, I don't worry much about what I wear or how I look to a passerby. In fact, I could only remember two passersby at Little Creek. One was a young fellow from down the road who had lost his coon dog. The other was an old man in a station wagon who was looking for a cabin where Hoagy Carmichael wrote some of his music. I hope by embracing solitude I am not just hiding. Yet, I know it is wrong to be selfish and aloof. I don't want to end up a loner who doesn't participate in community.

When I was a practicing surgeon, I refused to use a chain saw because I knew one slip could amputate a finger and put me out of business. Not that I don't still like my fingers, but being retired, a missing finger wouldn't matter nearly as much. In search of a saw, I drove to Bears, the local hardware store, where I get plenty of advice for all my projects, along with a free bag of popcorn. John, the power saw specialist, recommended a Stihl saw. I chose a lightweight model with a fourteen-inch guide bar, small enough that an aging woodcutter like myself could handle it safely, yet big enough to fell a decent-sized tree.

After coffee, I went to the barn. I found a pair of safety glasses and leather work gloves. I lifted the saw from its orange carrying case. With my hand, I brushed acrid-smelling ladybugs from the workbench and placed the saw there. To a woodcutter, his saw is a serious matter, the way a scalpel once was to me. I tested the amount of tension on the chain because I knew a loose chain could derail and whip around dangerously. I made sure the oil and gas tanks were full. I carefully felt a length of chain. The saw's sharp teeth pricked my finger. In a wooden cart with bicycle tires, I placed the saw, a heavy maul, and a splitting wedge. Pulling the cart like a coolie, I set out on the gravel lane through the woods. Acorns and hickory nuts fell like hailstones. Leaves sifted down and crunched underfoot. A cold tailwind blew behind my ears and on my neck. I kept looking up, hoping to see the barred owl that nested nearby. Fickle Mother Nature wouldn't allow me a glimpse of him.

There was no reason to fell a live tree because there was enough down wood in Little Creek's forest to heat the entire town of Nashville for a winter. Before long, I came across a hickory tree of the proper diameter. The shagbark had been on the ground a couple of years. Its wood was well seasoned but not yet rotting. Being hickory, it was guaranteed to burn with a nice scent. I was glad to find the tree near the road. I wouldn't have far to carry the logs.

I checked the stability of the trunk to be sure it wouldn't roll as I worked. Even though I found it well anchored, I stood on the uphill side of the log just in case it moved. I pulled the starter rope, and the saw roared to life. The exhaust belched blue smoke. I disengaged the chain break and revved the motor like a motorcyclist revving his Harley. I felt red-blooded and virile with a chain saw in my hands.

Cutting a tree into lengths is called "bucking." I wanted to buck chunks that would fit easily into the cabin's woodstove. I eyeballed an eighteen-inch section of the log and began the first cut. I let the weight of the saw carry the bite through the wood.

FIRE

A rooster tail of sawdust spewed from the chain. A burnt wood scent came to me. The log screeched in protest. With a firm grip on the saw's handle, I stayed alert to the tip of the blade to avoid a dangerous kickback, which would flip the whirling chain at me. A man could lose his nose in an instant. The log was supported at both ends, so I knew the blade would be pinched if I used a single cut from the top. I cut downward one-third of the thickness and finished with an up-cut. My second cut produced a nice length of firewood that brought a slight smile to my face.

After I bucked ten sections, my shirt was damp with sweat. Sawdust clung to the fabric. Fatigue began to weight my arms. The saw grew heavy and harder to handle. I knew the chance of a mishap was greater when I was tired. Weary, I switched off the motor and set the saw down. I was careful to avoid dulling the chain by letting it touch the ground.

For a few minutes, I relaxed on a log, regaining my strength. I watched a gray squirrel gather nuts in his mouth to fuel his own internal fire. He scrambled up the trunk of a beech tree and leapt from bough to bough in a thrilling high-wire act.

"Quick, quick, quick," the squirrel chortled, warning me that he and I should hurry up and get ready for the cold winter days ahead.

But I didn't feel that sense of urgency. I had begun to understand that life was better unhurried. Especially in the woods.

When I felt rested, I finished by cutting five more sections and several lengths of small limbs to use for kindling. I loaded the logs onto the cart and pulled it toward the cabin. The road was uphill. The wood was heavy. My thigh muscles strained to keep the cart rolling. I felt like an old mule must feel pulling a plow. Although I tried to keep myself reasonably fit, and I took no medication, my body wasn't what it once was. Tennis elbow, lumbosacral strain, trochanteric bursitis, rotator cuff tear, an old football knee. Something was always inflamed and sore, but I tried not to give in to it. My daddy taught me that. Life at Little Creek, however, is physically taxing. I worry about how long Toni and I will be able to take care of the cabin and the land. I often think that if we could just get ten more years, I would be satisfied. I have to keep telling myself, however, to accept what today will give me and to let tomorrow and next year take care of themselves. I guess that is what faith is about.

FIRE

I stacked the wood by the gravel lane away from the cabin so termites and carpenter ants from the logs wouldn't infest the house. When finished, I stepped back and looked at what I had accomplished. It was just a woodpile, not a piece of sculpture or even a stone wall, but it was satisfying to see nonetheless. There is an adage that wood you cut yourself warms you twice, once when you cut it and once when you burn it. I would add a third time—when you see your ricks neatly stacked.

Thursday, October twentieth. A gray, nippy morning. Through the window over the sink, I checked the thermometer and saw that it was thirty-eight degrees outside. Toni was still asleep with a comforter over her and Oscar on the bed beside her. I went to my bathroom in the back of the cabin. My nose was cold. My breath condensed on the mirror. I brushed my teeth and put a cup of dog food in Oscar's dish, the salmon-anchovy blend that Toni insists Oscar prefers to the duck. In the kitchen, I started a pot of coffee, making it strong. Now it was time to build a fire to take the chill out of the air and reap the heat of my labor in the forest.

The wood-burning stove sits on a brick hearth in the middle of the main room so heat radiates from it and circulates throughout the cabin. The stove is a simple and efficient machine with no moving parts except its door. It is just a rectangular cast-iron box on legs with a flue that rises straight up through the ceiling to the chimney.

While I waited for the coffee, I adjusted the damper to let in air for combustion. On a bed of cold ashes, I made a nest of newspaper and kindling. I went to the woodpile and selected two of the hickory logs I had cut. On the dam below, two whitetail does wearing dark winter coats grazed on the grass. For a few seconds they looked up at me with their big eyes, and I looked down at them. Then, full of grace and beauty, they turned and loped into the woods. Nature was practicing sleight of hand. Now you see it, now you don't. I was sorry to have interrupted their breakfast but grateful to have seen these creatures if only for a brief moment.

Back inside, I lighted the paper and waited for the kindling to ignite. Soon a fire began to sizzle and pop. I laid on the hickory. Flames licked the logs and danced up the flue with a roar. Although I could feel its heat, the fire wasn't matter as other elements like stone and water are. Fire is a manifestation of matter changing forms. Oxygen and carbon molecules united. They were transformed magically into something gaseous that gave off heat and light.

A fire can be beautiful or frightening, can bring you comfort or do you harm. In Vietnam I had seen flames from candles in a Cao Dau temple and flames from napalm in a scorched village. To Dante, hell was an inferno. To Shakespeare, love was a fire.

That morning I sat on the couch in front of the stove with its door open. I could see the flames, scintillating yellow, orange, and blue. The dark, warm scent of hickory smoke filled the room. Heat came slowly into my body. I started my day warmed.

*A man should be in the world as though he were
not in it, so that it will be no worse because of his life.
He is under obligation to leave it better than he found it.*

WENDELL BERRY
The Long-Legged House

DEPARTURE

November arrived too soon at Little Creek. The chickadees had refeathered for the winter. The coats of deer had turned gray. The days had shortened and shadows had lengthened. Another autumn had passed, leaving its residue of empty nutshells, fallen leaves, naked branches, and remembrances of the summer's warm days. It was tempting to stay in Indiana, to stoke the woodstove, read in front of a fire, hike over hills blanketed by fresh snow. Before long, however, the steep road to the cabin would be glazed with ice, unplowable and impassible. Although I knew each movement of the year had its own beauty, I had lost my tolerance for cold winds and the endless gray of winter. It was time to pack up and head south to our home in Boca Grande, off the gulf coast of Florida. There a more social, less elemental life awaited. But Boca Grande had much to offer, too: pure sunlight, salt water, sunsets, tropical birds, and friends we missed.

The day before we were to leave, Rick Ryan drove out to Little Creek in his old white van. He came to winterize the cabin and barn and to carry in things that were too heavy for me. Rick was in good spirits, anticipating deer season and a new job building a deck. When I asked him how he was feeling, he shrugged. With a guarded smile, he said his platelet count was low but holding its own. He was feeling okay. I wasn't totally convinced.

Toni boxed up her paints and brushes. She tackled the kitchen, cleaning out the refrigerator and pantry and putting away dishes. Rick and I shut off the water to the studio and outdoor shower. We used an old vacuum sweeper as an air compressor to blow out the pipes. Then we filled the drain traps with antifreeze. With Oscar barking at him, Rick put on knee pads. Like a bearded spelunker, he crawled under the house to cover vents with screening to keep out the critters. Porch furniture, my hammock, flowerpots, and the Walker Bay dinghy were stowed in the barn.

I knew it was best to live timelessly without longing. But as I uprooted the tomatoes, peppers, marigolds, and squash plants that had withered in the garden, I couldn't help feel nostalgia for last spring. I deposited the dead specimens in the Earth Machine to decompose over the winter. There was something spiritual about the making of compost—fertility arising from death—the past becoming the future. I stirred in wet leaves and planned what I would plant on our return next spring.

After a lunch of turkey breast and Swiss cheese sandwiches on the porch, Rick and I hiked down to a giant beech that had fallen near the pond. I had asked Rick to bring his chain saw, which had a longer blade than mine. We used it to cut thick slabs of wood from the trunk (the job Bill Poole had turned down). We lugged the round blocks of hardwood to the barn to season over the winter in anticipation of my sanding and oiling them and turning them into tabletops. The pergola that covered the path to the dock was dilapidated and rotting. The last time I was in New York visiting my daughter Katie, I had seen an appealing gate in the Chinese garden at the Metropolitan Museum of Art. Rick and I discussed how we could build something similar. In my mind, I planned a low stone wall that I would construct in front of the porch and backfill, then plant with shrubbery. I hoped I would be healthy and strong enough to lift the stones and shovel the earth as I had done the past summer. The dual process of remembering and planning made me feel as if I were looking back on tomorrow.

Toni had arranged with Susan Threehawk's cleaning service to check on the cabin while we were gone. Rick agreed to be available for repairs and to clear the road of trees that might fall and block its gravel surface. Toni piled him high with grocery sacks filled with vegetables, cheeses, meats, bread, and milk and sent him on his way. I hoped Rick's bone marrow would behave.

Toni and I spent the rest of the day preparing for our morning departure. We took a load of newspapers, magazines, and bottles to the recycling center in Nashville, garbage bags of trash to a dumpster at Bears, books to the library. The woodpile was depleted, so I cut a rick of hickory and stacked it for burning on the cool days of our return. On the hillside behind the cabin, I broadcast a blend of wildflower seeds. I hoped they would germinate and take root after the spring thaw. I took down bird feeders from the porch's eaves. I spread the remaining seeds on the ground, a last supper for our feathered friends.

Suitcases, the oil paintings Toni wanted to sell at a winter show in Florida, books and magazines to read on the road, the leather-bound volume of my haiku and Toni's watercolors, and Oscar's bed were carried to Toni's car. We were taking away less than we brought, leaving things like a good scout leaves his campsite, better than we found it when we came. I believed sincerely that for the most part we had fulfilled our obligation to the land.

Toni had plenty of advice about where our belongings should go inside the car, but I considered myself a superior packer-of-cars. I told her too many cooks spoiled the soup. She told me to do it my way as long as I allowed an acre of room for Oscar on the seat behind us.

In the retracting light of early evening, I put on a warm sweater and a ball cap. I selected a walking stick from our collection and set out for a last lap on the path through the woods and around the ponds. The clouds were the color of smoke, the ground shadows longer and less sharp than they were a month ago. The air was cold and pure. To inhale it was like taking a sip of fine chilled wine. Near the trailhead was the cairn Katie and her urologist husband, Eli, had built. Eli had named the stack of stones "Paradox" because it appeared stable but wasn't. I couldn't help smile, thinking life, like the cairn, wasn't always what it seemed.

Most of the leaves were down, and the trail offered a stunning view of dormant golden cornfields to the north of Bean Blossom Creek. In the distance, I saw the white clapboard houses of Helmsburg. The tin roof of Poole's sawmill glinted in dying light. The earth with its beauty, mystery, and dignity caused a slight chill to run up the back of my neck.

On the dam of the lower pond, I paused to sit on the bench. I remembered the floodwaters, fly fishing from the canoe, Toni's grandchildren feeding the catfish, Uncle Puff catching a bluegill. The image of the frightened doe in watery flight still unsettled me.

Sunlight shone through the trees at a low winter angle. It played on the water and lit up the wild grass on the shore. From above came the call of my high-flying friend, the red-tailed hawk. Soon an early milky moon shone in a steel-blue sky. As I often do when I look at the moon, I thought again of Neil Armstrong and how small the earth must have looked to him. It made me feel like a tiny no-see-um on the planet's skin.

Two weeks earlier, Toni and I had driven to the Morrison Woods nursing home in Muncie. It was our final visit with my sister and my father before we headed south. Now, as I sat on the bench looking at the moon and water, I thought of Daddy, red-eyed and shriveled in his wheelchair, a blanket on his lap. He was locked in a world without memory or any meaning as far as I could tell. I wondered if it would be the last time I saw him alive. Although I knew it would break my heart, I wanted him to go, to be free of suffering and loneliness.

I thought of my daughter Beth, pregnant with twins that would be born before it was time for me to return to Indiana next spring. Death and birth. Something lost, something gained. The cycle of the seasons. The immortality of gardens. There was much to marvel about the way the world perpetuates itself. I rose from the bench and headed up the hill to the cabin in a state of reverence.

It was still dark when Toni's iPhone alarm awakened us with the sound of a barking dog. I rose from the bed, groggy from a night wrestling with concerns about the trip ahead. The weather. The traffic. The car. What had I forgotten to do? I dressed in khakis and a cotton sweater that I had laid out before we went to bed. I brushed my teeth with bottled water. The cabin was so cold I could see my breath in the moonlight.

DEPARTURE

I wanted to build a fire in the stove, brew a pot of coffee, and settle onto the love seat with a book and flames to watch. But it was time to go. Life was moving on.

While Toni settled Oscar on his bed in the car, I went from room to room in dim light, testing the locks on windows and doors. I worried about break-ins and vandalism. But there was nothing to be gained by fretting about what was beyond my control. From the woodstove came the dank smell of ashes. The house was as silent and empty as my father's nursing home at night. I took my time, savoring a last look at things, imprinting them in memory: Toni's painting of birch trees, Mother's Waterford chandelier, the red Mongolian chest, the collection of carved birds, the log table I made of walnut, the sumptuous cherry floors and sturdy poplar walls. I seldom thought of my house on Riverside Drive and the life I left behind. I had more than enough at Little Creek. Blame was fading into understanding. A door had been opened to forgiveness. I stepped out into the gray of dawn. I put a key in the lock and turned it.

I slid into the car on a cold leather seat. I started the engine and glanced at Toni. She smiled tentatively. We were both quiet, suspended for the moment between the past and the future. I dropped the car into gear and headed down the lane. The tires growled on gravel. The headlights flashed through the trees. We rounded a turn in the road. In the rearview mirror, the cabin with its dark windows disappeared. We continued through the woods, where deer and turkeys were reclaiming what was theirs.

To have been at one with the earth, seems beyond undoing.

RAINER RILKE

EPILOGUE

Late on a soft blue afternoon in March, Toni and I were in Florida, preparing to take Oscar to the beach for a sunset romp when the telephone rang. It was my oldest daughter, Beth, calling from the obstetrical ward at St. Vincent's Women's Hospital in Indianapolis. In a worried voice, she told me her blood pressure was elevated and she was spilling protein into her urine. Although it was early in the eighth month of her pregnancy and an ultrasound estimated the twins' weights at slightly over three pounds each, her obstetrician had decided to deliver the babies that night by Cesarean section. From my days as a med student on the obstetrical service at the charity hospital in Indianapolis, I recognized the signs and symptoms of preeclampsia. Immediately, my mind filled with the complications of pregestational hypertension: seizures, diabetes, kidney damage, blood clots. And the complications of major surgery: hemorrhage, injury to ureters and bowel, cardiac arrest. One drawback to being a physician when your family is ill is that you know too much. I tried to sound calm. I told Beth everything would be fine. I would book the next morning flight to Indianapolis.

The twins were born surgically that evening: Teri Marie at 5:34 PM, Jacqueline

EPILOGUE

Jane at 5:36 PM. Soon after the delivery, Beth's husband, Chris, called to tell me the babies were doing well in the neonatal intensive care unit. Beth had come through the surgery without incident. Toni and I uncorked a bottle of Cakebread Chardonnay to celebrate the arrival of my first grandchildren. I had trouble falling asleep that night thinking of the life that lay ahead for the little girls. What would their aspirations be? Would they be fulfilled? Who would they become? Would they find happiness?

When I arrived at St. Vincent's the next day, Beth lay on her hospital bed in a pink housecoat. Her face and hands were swollen with edema fluid. Through a tube in her arm, a solution of magnesium sulfate dripped into her vein to control her blood pressure. She was pale and exhausted. But she smiled, and her face glowed. Beth had wanted a child so badly. She had been through so much to get pregnant, with hormone injections in her abdomen and attempts at in vitro fertilization. I kissed her, told her how proud I was of her, told her I knew she would be a good mother. Those are things one says, but they have never been more heartfelt.

Behind her on the windowsill was a pink carnation made to look like a scoop of strawberry ice cream in a cone. The card said, "Love Grammy Daniel," Daniel being the new surname of my former wife. Jane had remarried recently. The world had changed fast.

With her obstetrician's permission, I pushed Beth in a wheelchair to the neonatal intensive care. At the entryway, we scrubbed our hands with surgical soap. Electric-eye doors sprung open. I rolled Beth into a large room lined with rows of incubators tended by nurses in blue scrubs. Monitors chirped. Chimes rang over an intercom to announce the birth of another child. There was an assembly line feel to the operation. My heart was pounding.

We went first to Jacqueline's incubator, which was covered with a quilt. Cheryl, a nurse whose graying hair was plaited into dreadlocks, removed the quilt. There was Jacqueline, tiny and naked except for a diaper. Her arms and legs were bird-thin, her toes and fingers long and perfectly shaped. Her face was pretty and pink. She had a high Walker forehead and round cheeks. A plastic clamp clipped to the remnant of her umbilical cord reminded me of the miracle of fetal circulation, the sharing of blood and oxygen between mother and child. Jacqueline opened her eyes and looked at me. I felt a tightness in my throat and chest. I thought I might be suffocated by emotion.

Cheryl picked Jacqueline up and placed her in Beth's lap. She poured a thimble-sized portion of formula into a nippled bottle and handed it to Beth. Smiling warmly, the nurse showed Beth how to squeeze Jacqueline's cheeks to make her suck. While Beth fed Jacqueline, I studied the baby's vital signs that scrolled across the monitor's screen above her. The rate of her respirations was a rapid forty times a minute, compared to an adult's sixteen. Her blood pressure was a mere 66 over 45. Jacqueline's tiny heart raced along 150 times a minute. I thought of the hummingbirds at Little Creek. I could feel my own heart thudding.

With my iPhone, I snapped a picture of Beth and Jacqueline. Then I moved around the partition that separated her from her twin sister. My first sight of Teri, even tinier than Jacqueline, almost stopped my heart. Her eyes were covered with a black foam mask to protect her corneas from the ultraviolet light used to treat her neonatal jaundice. She looked like a tiny Zorro. A feeding tube protruded from the corner of her mouth. An intravenous line in her tiny arm provided the fluids and calories she would need until she was strong enough to nurse. I studied her diagnostically, looking for any congenital abnormalities—extra fingers, epicanthal folds, blue lips. I was relieved to see that everything about her was normal, just miniature. Her movements were small and writhing. Her lips pursed as if she dreamed of suckling. I could see she was in a struggle to survive. I remembered my daughter, Sarah, struggling in the same way when she was born with spina bifida. I wanted desperately to help Teri just as I had wanted so desperately to help Sarah. But there was nothing I could do. I felt powerless.

Beth, in her wheelchair, joined me at Teri's side. She opened the incubator's portal and reached into the clear plastic cube. She touched the baby's arm. A shiver passed through Teri's body. Her extremities jerked. Her whole body trembled in the warm air. Beth looked up at me with concern.

"Don't worry," I said. "It's a normal reflex in a newborn."

Beth stroked Teri's forehead with her index finger.

"Hi. Hi, baby girl," she said tenderly. "Sweet little baby. There you are."

Another shudder passed through Teri's tiny body.

EPILOGUE

"Yes," Beth whispered to her. "There you are. You're all right."

Not only I had met my granddaughters for the first time, I saw my daughter in a way I never had before. My eyes welled up.

On Saturday morning, I took a break from the hospital and drove through a light rain to Muncie to visit my father. Because of his progressive mental and physical deterioration, the Morrison Woods memory care unit was no longer able to care for him. He had been transferred to the health care center of Westminster, another nursing home in the area.

When I arrived at the door of his room, it was near noon. Daddy was still in bed. He lay on his back with his eyes closed and his mouth open. His hair swirled around his head like thin white smoke given off by smoldering dreams. His skin was wrinkled and so pale it appeared transparent. For a moment, I was startled. I thought he was dead. But as I moved closer, he took a breath.

"It's me, Daddy," I said, bending over him. He smelled sour like decay. "It's Daly."

He opened his watery red-rimmed gray eyes. He looked at me with a puzzled expression.

"It's Daly," I repeated.

He broke into a smile, showing yellow snaggled teeth.

"Daly," he said.

He held up both of his hands.

"Yes," I said. "It's me, Daly."

I took his left hand in mine. The absence of his watch on his wrist reminded me of the irrelevance of time in his life. I will never forget how soft his skin felt. It was a hand of total dependency, like the hands of Teri and Jacqueline. A week ago he had turned ninety-six. I thought of the near century his life had spanned, all he had seen, all the changes the world had made. His weary heart must have longed to stop. I took my iPhone from my pocket. On its screen, I showed him the photographs I had taken of the twins. I explained that they were his new great-granddaughters and that Beth had delivered them. Beth was his first grandchild. She called him "Boo." He had adored her.

EPILOGUE

"What do I do now?" he asked.

"Nothing," I said. The emptiness of his once full mind made me sad. "Just take it easy."

I sat with him for a while, answering repetitive inquiries about what he was to do. I thought back over the years we spent together, Mother, Sandra, and I, our modest sunlit house in Winchester. Daddy was such a kind and gentle man, a good father. I wished the twins could have known him. I wished he could hold them in his arms. He would have liked that more than anything. Before long, he dozed off. I left the room and went to the nurses' station to be sure they had the right phone number to reach me when the time came. I passed Daddy's door on the way out and heard him calling,

"Sandra. Daly. Sandra. Daly. Sandra. Daly. Sandra. Daly."

I quickened my steps and hurried out of the building.

Early the next morning, the day before I was to fly back to Florida, I set out in my rental car toward Brown County to check on our cabin. I wanted to determine how the property had survived the winter. I had spent the night with my daughter, Sarah, in her comfortable bungalow in the Fall Creek Place neighborhood of Indianapolis. She loaned me Jules, her companion dog, for the trip to Little Creek. The handsome mix of Labrador retriever and English setter had a shiny black coat. He looked at me with soulful big eyes. Loyal and obedient, Jules brought Sarah things she couldn't reach and helped pull her chair up ramps. I wouldn't tell Oscar, but Jules is the best dog I've known.

Frost whitened the ground, but the air was almost balmy, the sky clear and blue. As I pulled onto the interstate and headed south, tall buildings flickered past at seventy miles per hour. I imagined taking the twins by the hand and walking with them on the path through the woods at Little Creek. I would tell them the names of trees and explain the meaning of clouds and the nature of their impermanence. In the backseat, Jules snored gently in his sleep.

At Little Creek, I unlocked the front door and entered the cabin. Seen this way, dark and empty, silent, a bit musty, it was like an old resort hotel closed for the season.

EPILOGUE

I made my way from room to room. My mind replayed memories of last summer: making sauce with homegrown tomatoes while Toni boiled the spaghetti, stoking the stove with wood I had cut, oiling the walnut table, writing this memoir. Except for a fine film of dust on surfaces, everything was just as we had left it.

I locked up the cabin and climbed the steps to the barn's loft. The brightness of March sunlight filled Toni's studio. I looked at her oil paintings of Indiana barns and fields, the paintings that appear on these pages. Toni's absence was palpable. A feeling of lonesomeness came over me. On the floor, dead flies were scattered about. I swept up the carcasses and threw them into the woods, returned them to the earth. From the deck, I called Toni on my cell phone and told her all was well at Little Creek and with the twins. I told her she was missed.

Before I left, I walked down the hill to the dam between the ponds with Jules at my side. Thawed ground squished under my feet. Wet grass gave the earth a buoyancy. The dog leapt into the pond. While he swam, I drank in the landscape's collage of browns—the dark sepia of last year's leaves, the khaki water that filled the pond, the muddy brown of tree bark, the dark umber of wet stone walls. Even the air smelled brown. A profound silence gripped me. It was as if the world were holding its breath, about to exhale.

My mind returned to the twins. I pictured them, pink and tiny in their incubators. I thought how simple and elemental life is at the beginning. Ultraviolet light shined on their skin to clear their neonatal jaundice. While their immature lungs developed, air enriched with oxygen was fed to them. Heat radiated from the electric fire of the incubators and warmed them. Their formula, a product of the earth by way of grass and cows and soybeans, nourished them. Water from a plastic bag flowed into their veins, a stream of calories, minerals, and electrolytes to sustain them. Beth's milk was like rain from a cloud, so that what was her, who was me, became them.

On my way up the hill to the cabin, I noticed the shoots of crocuses that had broken ground and formed a spiky green circle in brown grass. The infantile flowers seemed to promise a future where they would become what they were intended to be, to grow and thrive and live out their days as fate would have it. I felt one with the earth.

ACKNOWLEDGMENTS

I am grateful to many people for this book. I would like to thank my publishers Nancy and Art Baxter, book designer Paul Wilson, and editor Rachel Popma. Special thanks goes to Lucinda Dickson Sullivan and Fred Bales for their intuitive insights, thoughtful editing, and enduring friendships. Also I would like to extend thanks to Barb Shoup, Sena Jeter Naslund, Sandra Kelly, Nancy Kriplen, Alice Gorman, Jane Geniesse, Tom McGuane, Bill Pierce, and Lou Ann Walker for their support and encouragement through the years.

ABOUT THE AUTHOR AND ARTIST

 Daly Walker, a retired surgeon, is a native of Indiana. His stories and essays have appeared in numerous literary publications, including the *Atlantic Monthly*, the *Sewanee Review*, the *Louisville Review*, the *Sycamore Review*, and the *Southampton Review*. His fiction has been anthologized in *Faith Stories*, *Story Matters*, and the *Bedford Introduction to Literature*. His collection of short stories, *Surgeon Stories*, was published by Fleur de Lis Press in 2011. Daly's work has been shortlisted for *The Best American Short Stories* and an O. Henry Award and was a finalist in *The Best American Magazine Writing*.

Toni Wolcott is originally from Connecticut. She is an interpretive painter who works in oils, watercolors, and pastels. Her subject matter includes classical botanicals, landscapes and seascapes, and structures of architectural interest. A graduate of Skidmore College, she has studied at the Ringling School of Art and Design and the Rochester Institute of Technology. She is an exhibiting member of the Boca Grande Art Alliance.